PART I

CIVILIZATION AND PROGRESS

HISTORY OF HUMAN SOCIETY

CHAPTER I

WHAT IS CIVILIZATION?

The Human Trail.—The trail of human life beginning in the mists of the past, winding through the ages and stretching away toward an unknown future, is a subject of perennial interest and worthy of profound thought. No other great subject so invites the attention of the mind of man. It is a very long trail, rough and unblazed, wandering over the continents of the earth. Those who have travelled it came in contact with the mysteries of an unknown world. They faced the terrors of the shifting forms of the earth, of volcanoes, earthquakes, floods, storms, and ice fields. They witnessed the extinction of forests and animal groups, and the changing forms of lakes, rivers, and mountains, and, indeed, the boundaries of oceans.

It is the trail of human events and human endeavor on which man developed his physical powers, enlarged his brain capacity, developed and enriched his mind, and became efficient through art and industry. Through inventions and discovery he turned the forces of nature to his use, making them serve his will. In association with his fellows, man learned that mutual aid and co-operation were necessary to the survival of the race. To learn this caused him more trouble than all the terrors and mysteries of the natural world around him. Connected with the trail is a long chain of causes and effects, trial and error, success and failure, out of which has come the advancement of the race. The accumulated results of life on the trail are called *civilization*.

Civilization May Be Defined.—To know what civilization is by study and observation is better than to rely upon a formal definition. For, indeed, the word is used in so many different ways that it admits of a loose interpretation. For instance, it may be used in a narrow sense to indicate the character and quality of the civil relations. Those tribes or nations having a well-developed social order, with government, laws, and other fixed social customs, are said to be civilized, while those peoples without these characters are assumed to be uncivilized. It may also be considered in a somewhat different sense, when the arts, industries, sciences, and habits of life are stimulated—civilization being determined by the degree in which these are developed. Whichever view is accepted, it involves a contrast of present ideals with past ideals, of an undeveloped with a developed state of human progress.

But whatever notion we have of civilization, it is difficult to draw a fixed line between civilized and uncivilized peoples. Mr. Lewis H. Morgan, in his *Ancient Society*, asserts that civilization began with the phonetic alphabet, and that all human activity prior to this could be classified as savagery or barbarism. But there is a broader conception of civilization which recognizes all phases of human achievement, from the making of a stone axe to the construction of the airplane; from the rude hut to the magnificent palace; from crude moral and religious conditions to the more refined conditions of human association. If we consider that civilization involves the whole process of human achievement, it must admit of a great variety of qualities and degrees of development, hence it appears to be a relative term applied to the variation of human life. Thus, the Japanese are highly civilized along special lines of hand work, hand industry, and hand art, as well as being superior in some phases of family relationships. So we might say of the Chinese, the East Indians, and the American Indians, that they each have well-established customs, habits of thought, and standards of life, differing from other nations, expressing different types of civilization.

When a member of a primitive tribe invented the bow-and-arrow, or began to chip a flint nodule in order to make a stone axe, civilization began. As soon as people began to co-operate with one another in obtaining food, building houses, or for protection against wild animals and wild men, that is, when they began to treat each other civilly, they were becoming civilized. We may say then in reality that civilization has been a continuous process from the first beginning of man's conquest of himself and nature to the modern complexities of social life with its multitude of products of industry and cultural arts.

It is very common for one group or race to assume to be highly civilized and call the others barbarians or savages. Thus the Hebrews assumed superiority when they called other people Gentiles, and the Greeks when they called others barbarians. Indeed, it is only within recent years that we are beginning to recognize that the civilizations of China, Japan, and India have qualities worth studying and that they may have something worth while in life that the Western civilization has not. Also there has been a tendency to confuse the terms Christian and heathen with civilized and uncivilized. This idea arose in England, where, in the early history of Christianity, the people of the towns were more cultured than the people of the country.

It happened, too, that the townspeople received Christianity before the people of the country, hence heathens were the people who dwelt out on the heath, away from town. This local idea became a world idea when all non-Christian peoples were called uncivilized. It is a fatal error for an individual, neighborhood, tribe, or nation to assume superiority to the extent that it fails to recognize good qualities in others. One should not look with disdain upon a tribe of American Indians, calling them uncivilized because their material life is simple, when in reality in point of honor, faithfulness, and courage they excel a large proportion of the races assuming a higher civilization.

The Material Evidences of Civilization Are All Around Us.—Behold this beautiful valley of the West, with its broad, fertile fields, yielding rich harvests of corn and wheat, and brightened by varied forms of fruit and flower. Farmhouses and schoolhouses dot the landscape, while towns and cities, with their marts of trade and busy industries, rise at intervals. Here are churches, colleges, and libraries, indicative of the education of the community; courthouses, prisons, and jails, which speak of government, law, order, and protection. Here are homes for the aged and weak, hospitals and schools for the defective, almshouses for the indigent, and reformatories for the wayward. Railroads bind together all parts of the nation, making exchange possible, and bringing to our doors the products of every clime. The telephone and the radio unite distant people with common knowledge, thought, and sentiment. Factories and mills line the streams or cluster in village and city, marking the busy industrial life. These and more mark the visible products of civilization.

But civilization is something more than form, it is spirit; and its evidence may be more clearly discerned in the co-operation of men in political organization and industrial life, by their united action in religious worship and charitable service, in social order and educational advancement. Observe, too, the happy homes, with all of their sweet and hallowed influences, and the social mingling of the people searching for pleasure or profit in their peaceful, harmonious association. Witness the evidences of accumulated knowledge in newspapers, periodicals, and books, and the culture of painting, poetry, and music. Behold, too, the achievements of the mind in the invention and discovery of the age; steam and electrical appliances that cause the whirl of bright machinery, that turn night into day, and make thought travel swift as the wings of the wind! Consider the influence of chemistry, biology, and medicine on material welfare, and the discoveries of the products of the earth that subserve man's purpose! And the central idea of all this is man, who walks upright in the dignity and grace of his own manhood, surrounded by the evidence of his own achievements. His knowledge, his power of thought, his moral character, and his capacity for living a large life, are evidences of the real civilization. For individual culture is, after all, the flower and fruit, the beauty and strength of civilization.

One hundred years ago neither dwelling, church, nor city greeted the eye that gazed over the broad expanse of the unfilled prairies. Here were no accumulations of wealth, no signs of human habitation, except a few Indians wandering in groups or assembled in their wigwam villages. The evidences of art and industry were meagre, and of accumulated knowledge small, because the natives were still the children of nature and had gone but a little way in the mastery of physical forces or in the accumulation of knowledge. The relative difference in their condition and that of those that followed them is the contrast between barbarism and civilization.

Yet how rapid was the change that replaced the latter with the former. Behold great commonwealths built in half a century! What is the secret of this great and marvellous change? It is a transplanted civilization, not an indigenous one. Men came to this fertile valley with the spiritual and material products of modern life, the outcome of centuries of progress. They brought the results of man's struggle, with himself and with nature, for thousands of years. This made it possible to build a commonwealth in half a century. The first settlers brought with them a knowledge of the industrial arts; the theory and practice of social order; individual capacity, and a thirst for education. It was necessary only to set up the machinery already created, and civilization went forward. When they began the life of labor, the accumulated wealth of the whole world was to be had in exchange for the products of the soil.

Primitive Man Faced an Unknown World.—But how different is the picture of primitive man suddenly brought face to face with an unknown world. With no knowledge of nature or art, with no theory or practice of social order, he began to dig and to delve for the preservation of life. Suffering the pangs of hunger, he obtained food; naked, he clothed himself; buffeted by storm and wind and scorched by the penetrating rays of the sun, he built himself a shelter. As he gradually became skilled in the industrial arts, his knowledge increased. He formed a clearer estimate of how nature might serve him, and obtained more implements with which to work

The social order of the family and the state slowly appeared. Man became a co-operating creature, working with his fellows in the satisfaction of material wants and in protecting the rights of individuals. Slow and painful was this process of development, but as he worked his capacity enlarged, his power increased, until he mastered the forces of nature and turned them to serve him; he accumulated knowledge and brought forth culture and learning; he marshalled the social forces in orderly process. Each new mastery of nature or self was a power for the future, for civilization is cumulative in its nature; it works in a geometrical progression. An idea once formed, others follow; one invention leads to another, and each material form of progress furnishes a basis for a more rapid progress and for a larger life. The discovery and use of a new food product increased the power of civilization a hundredfold. One step in social order leads to another, and thus is furnished a means of utilizing without waste all of the individual and social forces.

Yet how irregular and faltering are the first steps of human progress. A step forward, followed by a long period of readjustment of the conditions of life; a movement forward here and a retarding force there. Within this irregular movement we discover the true course of human progress. One tribe, on account of peculiar advantages, makes a special discovery, which places it in the ascendancy and gives it power over others. It has obtained a favorable location for protection against oppressors or a fertile soil, a good hunting ground or a superior climate. It survives all opposing factors for a time, and, obtaining some idea of progress, it goes on adding strength unto strength, or is crowded from its favorable position by its warlike neighbors to perish from the earth, or to live a stationary or even a deteriorating life. A strong tribe, through internal development and the domination of other groups, finally becomes a great nation in an advanced state of civilization. It passes through the course of infancy, youth, maturity, old age, and death. But the products of its civilization are handed on to other nations. Another rises and, when about to enter an advanced state of progress, perishes on account of internal maladies. It is overshadowed with despotism, oppressed by priestcraft, or lacking industrial vitality to such a degree that it is forced to surrender the beginnings of civilization to other nations and other lives.

The dominance of a group is dependent in part on the natural or inherent qualities of mind and body of its members, which give it power to achieve by adapting itself to conditions of nature and in mastering and utilizing natural resources. Thus the tribe that makes new devices for procuring food or new weapons for defense, or learns how to sow seeds and till the soil, adds to its means of survival and progress and thus forges ahead of those tribes lacking in these means. Also the social heritage or the inheritance of all of the products of industry and arts of life which are passed on from generation to generation, is essential to the rapid development of civilization.

Civilization Is Expressed in a Variety of Ways.—Different ideals and the adaptation to different environment cause different types of life. The ideals of the Persian, the Greek, the Roman, and the Teuton varied. Still greater is the contrast between these and the Chinese and the Egyptian ideals. China boasts of an ancient civilization that had its origin long before the faint beginnings of Western nations, and the Chinese are firm believers in their own culture and superior advancement. The silent grandeur of the pyramids and temples of the Nile valley bespeak a civilization of great maturity, that did much for the world in general, but little for the Egyptian people. Yet these types of civilization are far different from that of Western nations. Their ideas of culture are in great contrast to our own. But even the Western nations are not uniform in ideals of civil life nor in their practice of social order. They are not identical in religious life, and their ideals of art and social progress vary.

Moreover, the racial type varies somewhat and with it the national life and thought. Compare England, Germany, France, and Spain as to the variability in characteristics of literature and art, in moral ideals, in ethical practice, in religious motive, and in social order. Their differences are evident, but they tend to disappear under the influence of rapid transit and close intercommunication, which draw all modern nations nearer together. Yet, granting the variability of ideals and of practice, there is a general consensus of opinion as to what constitutes civilization and what are the elements of progress. Modern writers differ somewhat in opinion as to elements of civilization, but these differences are more apparent than real, as all true civilization must rest upon a solid foundation of common human traits. The fundamental principles and chief characteristics are quite uniform for all nations and for all times, and writers who disagree as to general characteristics may not be classified by national boundaries; they represent the differences of philosophers.

Modern Civilization Includes Some Fundamentals.—As applied at different periods of the world's progress and as a representation of different phases of life, civilization means more to-day than ever before; its ideal is higher, its conception broader. In the modern, accepted sense it includes (1) *a definite knowledge of man and nature.* The classified knowledge of science and philosophy and all phases of the history of man socially and individually are important in estimating his true progress. All forms of thought and life are to be estimated in considering the full meaning of the term. It also includes (2) *progress in art.* While science deals with principles, art deals with rules of action. Science gives classified knowledge, while art directs to a practical end. Art provides definite plans how to operate. If these plans are carried out, the field of practice is entered. In its broadest conception art includes the making and the doing, as well as the plan. The fine arts and the industrial or practical arts, in all of their varied interests, are included in art as a factor in civilization. This category should include the highest forms of painting, poetry, sculpture, and music, as well as the lowest forms of industrial implements.

Civilization includes (3) *a well-developed ethical code* quite universally observed by a community or nation. The rule of conduct of man toward himself and toward his fellows is one of the essential points of discrimination between barbarism and civilization. While ethical practice began at a very early period in the progress of man, it was a long time before any distinct ethical code became established. But the completed civilization does not exist until a high order of moral practice obtains; no civilization can long prevail without it. Of less importance, but of no less binding force, is (4) the *social code,* which represents the forms and conventionalities of society, built, it is true, largely upon the caprices of fashion, and varying greatly in different communities, yet more arbitrary, if possible, than the moral code. It considers fitness and consistency in conduct, and as such is an important consideration in social usage and social progress. In Europe it has its extreme in the court etiquette; in America, in the punctiliousness of the higher social classes of our large cities. But it affects all communities, and its observance may be noted in rural districts as well as in the city population.

The mores, or customs, of man began at a very early time and have been a persistent ruling power in human conduct. Through tradition they are handed down from generation to generation, to be observed with more or less fidelity as a guide to the art of living. Every community, whether primitive or developed, is controlled to a great extent by the prevailing custom. It is common for individuals and families to do as their ancestors did. This habit is frequently carried to such an extent that the deeds of the fathers are held sacred from which no one dare to depart. Isolated communities continue year after year to do things because they had always done so, holding strictly to the ruling custom founded on tradition, even when some better way was at hand. A rare example of this human trait is given by Captain Donald MacMillan, who recently returned from Arctic Greenland. He said: "We took two ultra-modern developments, motion pictures and radio, direct to a people who live and think as their ancestors did two thousand years ago." He was asked: "What did they think?" He replied: "I do not know." Probably it was a case of wonder without thought. While this is a dominant force which makes for the unity and perpetuity of the group, it is only by departure from established tradition that progress is made possible.

Civilization involves (5) *government and law*. The tribes and nations in a state of barbarism lived under the binding influence of custom. In this period people were born under *status*, or condition, not under law. Gradually the old family life expanded into the state, and government became more formal. Law appeared as the expression of the will of the people directly or indirectly through their representatives. True, it may have been the arbitrary ruling of a king, but he represented the unity of the race and spoke with the authority of the nation. Law found no expression until there was formed an organic community capable of having a will respecting the control of those who composed it. It implies a governing body and a body governed; it implies an orderly movement of society according to a rule of action called law. While social order is generally obtained through law and government, such is the practice in modern life that the orderly association of men in trade and commerce and in daily contact appears to stand alone and to rise above the control of the law. Indeed, in a true civilization, the civil code, though an essential factor, seems to be outclassed by the higher social instincts based on the practice of social order.

(6) *Religion* must take a large place as a factor in the development of civilization. The character of the religious belief of man is, to a certain extent, the true test of his progressive nature. His faith may prove a source of inspiration to reason and progressive life; it may prove the opposite, and lead to stagnation and retrogression. Upon the whole, it must be insisted that religious belief has subserved a large purpose in the economy of human progress. It has been universal to all tribes, for even the lowest have some form of religious belief—at least, a belief in spiritual beings. Religious belief thus became the primary source of abstract ideas, and it has always been conducive to social order. It has, in modern times especially, furnished the foundation of morality. By surrounding marriage with ceremonies it has purified the home life, upheld the authority of the family, and thus strengthened social order. It has developed the individual by furnishing an ideal before science and positive knowledge made it possible. It strengthened patriotic feeling on account of service rendered in supporting local government, and subjectively religion improved man by teaching him to obey a superior. Again, by its tradition it frequently stifled thought and retarded progress.

Among other elements of civilization must be mentioned (7) *social well-being*. The preceding conditions would be almost certain to insure social well-being and prosperity. Yet it might be possible, through lack of harmony of these forces, on account of their improper distribution in a community, that the group might lack in general social prosperity. Unless there is general contentment and happiness there cannot be said to be an ideal state of civilization. And this social well-being is closely allied to (8) *material prosperity*, the most apparent element to be mentioned in the present analysis. The amount of the accumulation of the wealth of a nation, its distribution among the people, and the manner in which it is obtained and expended, determine the state of civilization. This material prosperity makes the better phases of civilization possible. It is essential to modern progress, and our civilization should seek to render it possible for all classes to earn their bread and to have leisure and opportunity for self-culture.

The mastery of the forces of nature is the basis for man's material prosperity. Touching nature here and there, by discovery, invention, and toil, causing her to yield her treasures for his service, is the key to all progress. In this, it is not so much conflict with nature as co-operation with her, that yields utility and eventually mastery. The discovery and use of new food products, the coal and other minerals of the earth, the forests, the water power and electric power, coupled with invention and adaptability to continually greater use, are the qualifying opportunity for advancement. Without these the fine theories of the philosopher, exalted religious belief, and high ideals of life are of no avail.

From the foregoing it may be said that civilization in its fulness means all of the acquired capabilities of man as evidenced by his conduct and the material products arising from his physical and mental exertion. It is evident that at first the structure called civilization began to develop very slowly and very feebly; just when it began it is difficult to state. The creation of the first utility, the first substantial movement to increase the food supply, the first home for protection, the first religious ceremony, or the first organized household, represents the beginnings of civilization, and these are the landmarks along the trail of man's ascendency.

Progress Is an Essential Characteristic of Civilization.—The goal is never reached, the victory is never finally achieved. Man must move on, ever on. Intellect must develop, morals improve, liberty increase, social order be perfected, and social growth continue. There must be no halting on the road; the nation that hesitates is lost. Progress in general is marked by the development of the individual, on the one hand, and that of society, on the other. In well-ordered society these two ideas are balanced; they seek an equilibrium. Excessive individualism leads to anarchy and destruction; excessive socialism blights and stagnates individual activity and independence and retards progress. It must be admitted here as elsewhere that the individual culture and the individual life are, after all, the highest aims. But how can these be obtained in modern life without social progress? How can there be freedom of action for the development of the individual powers without social expansion? Truly, the social and the individual life are complementary elements of progress.

Diversity Is Necessary to Progress.—If progress is an essential characteristic of modern civilization, it may be said that diversity is essential to progress. There is much said about equality and fraternity. It depends on what is meant by the terms as to whether these are good sayings or not. If equality means uniformity, by it man is easily reduced to a state of stagnation. Diversity of life exists everywhere in progressive nature, where plants or animals move forward in the scale of existence. Man is not an exception to the rule, notwithstanding his strong will force. Men differ in strength, in moral and intellectual capacity, and in co-operating ability. Hence they must occupy different stations in life. And the quality and quantity of progress are to be estimated in different nations according to the diversity of life to be observed among individuals and groups.

What Is the Goal of Civilized Man?—And it may be well to ask, as civilization is progressive: What is our aim in life from our own standpoint? For what do men strive? What is the ultimate of life? What is the best for which humanity can live? If it were merely to obtain food and clothes and nothing more, the question could be easily answered. If it were merely to train a man to be a monk, that he might spend his time in prayer and supplication for a better future life, the question would be simple enough. If to pore over books to find out the knowledge of the past and to spend the life in investigation of truth were the chief aims, it would be easy to determine the object of life. But frequently that which we call success in life is merely a means to an end.

And viewed in the complex activity of society, it is difficult to say what is the true end of life; it is difficult to determine the true end of civilization. Some have said it is found in administering the "greatest good to the greatest number," and if we consider in this the generations yet unborn, it reveals the actual tendency of modern civilization. If the perfection of the individual is the highest ideal of civilization, it stops not with one individual, but includes all. And this asserts that social well-being must be included in the final aim, for full and free individual development cannot appear without it. The enlarged capacity for living correctly, enjoying the best of this life righteously, and for associating harmoniously and justly with his fellows, is the highest aim of the individual. Happiness of the greatest number through utility is the formula for modern civilization.

Possibilities of Civilization.—The possibilities of reaching a still higher state of civilization are indeed great. The future is not full of foreboding, but bright and happy with promise of individual culture and social progress. If opportunities are but wisely used, the twentieth century will witness an advancement beyond our highest dreams. Yet the whole problem hinges on the right use of knowledge. If the knowledge of chemistry is to be used to destroy nations and races with gases and high explosives, such knowledge turns civilization to destruction. If all of the powers of nature under man's control should be turned against him, civilization would be turned back upon itself. Let us have "the will to believe" that we have entered an era of vital progress, of social improvement, of political reforms, which will lead to the protection of those who need protection and the elevation of those who desire it. The rapid progress in art and architecture, in invention and industry, the building of libraries and the diffusion of knowledge, the improvement of our educational system, all being entered upon, will force the world forward at a rapid pace, and on such a rational basis that the delight of living will be greatly enhanced for all classes.

Civilization Can Be Estimated.—This brief presentation of the meaning of civilization reveals the fact that civilization can be recounted; that it is a question of fact and philosophy that can be measured. It is the story of human progress and the causes which made it. It presents the generalizations of all that is valuable in the life of the race. It is the epitome of the history of humanity in its onward sweep. In its critical sense it cannot be called history, for it neglects details for general statements. Nor is it the philosophy of history, for it covers a broader field. It is not speculation, for it deals with fact. It is the philosophy of man's life as to the results of his activity. It shows alike the unfolding of the individual and of society, and it represents these in every phase embraced in the word "progress." To recount this progress and to measure civilization is the purpose of the following pages, so far as it may be done in the limited space assigned.

SUBJECTS FOR FURTHER STUDY

1. Are people of civilized races happier now than are the uncivilized races?

2. Would the American Indians in time have developed a high state of civilization?

3. Why do we not find a high state of civilization among the African negroes?

4. What are the material evidences of civilization in the neighborhood in which you live?

5. Does increased knowledge alone insure an advanced civilization?

6. Choose an important public building in your neighborhood and trace the sources of architecture of the different parts.

CHAPTER II

THE ESSENTIALS OF PROGRESS

How Mankind Goes Forward on the Trail.—Although civilization cannot exist without it, progress is something different from the sum-total of the products of civilization. It may be said to be the process through which civilization is obtained, or, perhaps more fittingly, it is the log of the course that marks civilization. There can be no conception of progress without ideals, which are standards set up toward which humanity travels. And as humanity never rises above its ideals, the possibilities of progress are limited by them. If ideals are high, there are possibilities of a high state of culture; if they are low, the possibilities are lessened, and, indeed, frequently are barren of results. But having established ideals as beacon lights for humanity to follow, the final test is whether there is sufficient knowledge, sufficient ability, and sufficient will-power to approximate them. In other words, shall humanity complete the trail of life, go on higher and higher grounds where are set the standards or goals to be reached; or will humanity rest easily and contentedly on a low level with no attempt to reach a higher level, or, indeed, will humanity, failing in desires for betterment, initiative, and will-power, drift to lower levels?

Groups, either tribes, races, or nations, may advance along given lines and be stationary or even retarded along other lines of development. If the accumulation of wealth is the dominant ideal, it may be so strenuously followed as to destroy opportunity for other phases of life. If the flow of energy is all toward a religious belief that absorbs the time and energy of people in the building of pyramids, mausoleums, cathedrals, and mosques, and taboos the inquiry into nature which might yield a large improvement in the race, religion would be developed at the expense of race improvement.

Change Is Not Necessarily Progress.—It is quite common in a popular sense for people to identify change with progress, or indeed to accept the wonderful changes which take place as causes of progress, when in reality they should have taken more care to search out the elements of progress of the great moving panorama of changing life. Changes are frequently violent, sudden, tremendous in their immediate effect. They move rapidly and involve many complexes, but progress is a slow-going old tortoise that plods along irrespective of storm or sunshine, life or death, of the cataclysms of war or the catastrophes of earthquakes or volcanoes. Progress moves slowly along through political and social revolutions, gaining a little here and a little there, and registering the things that are really worth while out of the ceaseless, changing humanity.

Achievement may take place without betterment, but all progress must make a record of betterment with achievement. A man may write a book or invent a machine at great labor. So far as he is concerned it is an achievement, but unless it is a good book, a good invention, better than others, so that they may be used for the advancement of the race, they will not form a betterment. Many of the changes of life represent the results of trial and error. "There is a way that seemeth right" to a nation which may end in destruction. The evil aroused is sometimes greater than the good. The prosperity of the Roman Empire was destroyed because of luxury and corrupt administration. The German Empire developed great powers in government, education, in the arts and sciences, but her military purpose nearly destroyed her. The Spanish Empire that once controlled a good part of the American continent failed because laborers were driven out of Spain and the wealth gained by exploitation was used to support the nobility and royalty in luxury. Whether the United States will continue to carry out her high purposes will depend upon the right use of her immense wealth and power. Likewise the radio, the movie, and the automobile are making tremendous changes. Will the opportunities they furnish improve the moral and intellectual character of the people—a necessary condition to real progress?

In considering modern progress, too frequently it is estimated by the greatness of things, by the stupendous changes, or by the marvellous achievements of the age, and we pause and wonder at what has been accomplished; but if we think long enough and clearly enough, we may get a vision of real progress, and we may find it difficult to determine the outcome of it all, so far as the real betterment of the race is concerned. Is the millionaire of to-day any happier, necessarily, and any more moral or of a higher religious standard than the primitive man or the savage of the plains or forest of to-day? True, he has power to achieve in many directions, but is he any happier or better? It may be said that his millions may accomplish great good. This is true if they are properly applied. It is also true that they are capable of great harm if improperly used.

As we stand and gaze at the movements of the airplane, or contemplate its rapid flight from ocean to ocean and from land to land around the world, we are impressed with this great wonder of the age, the great achievement of the inventive power of man. But what of the gain to humanity? If it is possible to transport the mails from New York to San Francisco in sixteen hours instead of in five days, is there advantage in that except the quickening process of transportation and life? Is it not worth while to inquire what the man at the other end of the line is going to do by having his mail four days ahead? He will hurry up somebody else and somebody else will hurry the next one, and we only increase the rapidity of motion. Does it really give us more time for leisure, and if so, are we using that leisure time in the development of our reflective intellectual powers or our spiritual life? It is easier to see improvement in the case of the radio, whereby songs and lectures can be broadcast all over the earth, and the community of life and the community of interest are developed thereby, and, also, the leisure hours are devoted to a contemplation of high ideals, of beautiful music, of noble thoughts. We do recognize a modicum of progress out of the great whirring, rapid changes in transportation and creative industry; but let us not be deceived by substituting change for progress, or making the two identical.

Thus human progress is something more than achievement, and it is something more than the exhibition of tools. It is determined by the use of the tools and involves betterment of the human race. Hence, all the products of social heredity, of language, of science, of religion, of art, and of government are progressive in proportion as they are successfully used for individual and social betterment. For if government is used to enslave people, or science to destroy them, or religion to stifle them, there can be no progress.

Progress Expresses Itself in a Variety of Ideals and Aims.—Progress involves many lines of development. It may include biological development of the human race, the development of man, especially his growth of brain power. It may consider man's adaptation to environment under different phases of life. It may consider the efficiency of bodily structure. In a cultural sense, progress may refer to the products of the industrial arts, or to the development of fine arts, or the advancement of religious life and belief —in fact, to the mastery of the resources of nature and their service to mankind in whatever form they may appear or in whatever phase of life they may be expressed. Progress may also be indicated in the improvement in social order and in government, and also the increased opportunity of the individual to receive culture through the process of mutual aid. In fact, progress must be sought for in all phases of human activity. Whatever phase of progress is considered, its line of demarcation is carefully drawn in the process of change from the old to the new, but the results of these changes will be the indices of either progress or retardation.

Progress of the Part and Progress of the Whole.—An individual might through hereditary qualities have superior mental traits or physical powers. These also may receive specific development under favorable educational environment, but the inertia of the group or the race might render ineffective a salutary use of his powers. A man is sometimes elected mayor of a town and devotes his energies to municipal betterment. But he may be surrounded by corrupt politicians and promoters of enterprises who hedge his way at every turn. Also, in a similar way, a group or tribe may go forward, and yet the products of its endeavor be lost to the world. Thus a productiveness of the part may be exhibited without the progress of the race. The former moves with concrete limitations, the latter in sweeping, cycling changes; but the latter cannot exist without the former, because it is from the parts that the whole is created, and it is the generalization of the accumulated knowledge or activities of the parts that makes it possible for the whole to develop.

The evolution of the human race includes the idea of differentiation of parts and a generalization that makes the whole of progress. So it is not easy to determine the result of a local activity as progressive until its relation to other parts is determined, nor until other activities and the whole of life are determined. Local colorings of life may be so provincial in their view-point as to be practically valueless in the estimation of the degree and quality of progress. Certain towns, especially in rural districts not acquainted with better things, boast that they have the best school, the best court-house, the best climate—in fact, everything best. When they finally awaken from their local dream, they discover their own deficiencies.

The great development of art, literature, philosophy, and politics among the ancient Greeks was inefficient in raising the great masses of the people to a higher plane of living, but the fruits of the lives of these superiors were handed on to other groups to utilize, and they are not without influence over the whole human group of to-day. So, too, the religious mystic philosophy and literature of India represented a high state of mental development, but the products of its existence left the races of India in darkness because the mystic philosophy was not adaptable to the practical affairs of life. The Indian philosophers may have handed on ideas which caused admiration and wonder, but they have had very little influence of a practical nature on Western civilization. So society may make progress in either art, religion, or government for a time, and then, for the want of adaptation to the conditions imposed by progress, the effects may disappear. Yet not all is lost, for some achievements in the form of tools are passed on through social heredity and utilized by other races. In the long run it is the total of the progress of the race, the progress of the whole, that is the final test.

Social Progress Involves Individual Development.—If we trace progress backward over the trail which it has followed, there are two lines of development more or less clearly defined. One is the improvement of the racial stock through the hereditary traits of individuals. The brain is enlarged, the body developed in character and efficiency, and the entire physical system has changed through variation in accordance with the laws of heredity. What we observe is development in the individual, which is its primary function. Progress in this line must furnish individuals of a higher type in the procession of the generations. The other line is through social heredity, that is the accumulated products of civilization handed down from generation to generation. This gives each succeeding generation a new, improved kit of tools, it brings each new generation into a better environment and surrounds it with ready-made means to carry on the improvement and add something for the use of the next generation. Knowledge of the arts and industries, language and books, are thus products of social heredity. Also buildings, machinery, roads, educational systems, and school buildings are inherited.

Connected with these two methods of development must be the discovery of the use of the human mind evidenced by the beginning of reflective thought. It is said by some writers that we are still largely in the age of instincts and emotions and have just recently entered the age of reason. Such positive statements should be considered with a wider vision of life, for one cannot conceive of civilization at all without the beginning of reflective mental processes. Simple inventions, like the use of fire, the bow-and-arrow, or the flint knife, may have come about primarily through the desire to accomplish something by subjecting means to an end, but in the perfection of the use of these things, which occurred very early in primitive life, there must have been reflective thinking in order to shape the knife for its purpose, make the bow-and-arrow more effective, and utilize fire for cooking, heating, and smelting. All of these must have come primarily through the individual initiative.

Frequent advocates of social achievement would lead one to suppose that the tribe in need of some method of cutting should assemble and pass the resolution that a flint knife be made, when any one knows it was the reflective process of the individual mind which sought adaptation to environment or means to accomplish a purpose. Of course the philosopher may read many generalizations into this which may confuse one in trying to observe the simple fact, for it is to be deplored that much of the philosophy of to-day is a smoke screen which obscures the simple truth.

The difference of races in achievement and in culture is traced primarily to hereditary traits developed through variation, through intrinsic stimuli, or those originating through so-called inborn traits. These traits enable some races to achieve and adapt themselves to their environment, and cause others to fail. Thus, some groups or races have perished because of living near a swamp infested with malaria-carrying mosquitoes or in countries where the food supply was insufficient. They lacked initiative to move to a more healthful region or one more bountiful in food products, or else they lacked knowledge and skill to protect themselves against mosquitoes or to increase the food supply. Moreover, they had no power within them to seek the better environment or to change the environment for their own advancement. This does not ignore the tremendous influence of environment in the production of race culture. Its influence is tremendous, especially because environmental conditions are more under the direction of intelligence than is the development of hereditary traits.

Some writers have maintained that there is no difference in the dynamic, mental, or physical power of races, and that the difference of races which we observe to-day is based upon the fact that some have been retarded by poor environment, and others have advanced because of fortunate environment. This argument is good as far as it goes, but it does not tell the whole story. It does not show why some races under good environment have not succeeded, while others under poor environment have succeeded well. It does not show why some races have the wit to change to a better environment or transform the old environment.

There seems to be a great persistency of individual traits, of family traits, and, in a still larger generalization, of racial traits which culture fails to obliterate. As these differences of traits seem to be universal, it appears that the particular combination which gives motor power may also be a differentiation. At least, as all races have had the same earth, why, if they are so equal in the beginning, would they not achieve? Had they no inventive power? Also, when these so-called retarded races came in contact with the more advanced races who were superior in arts and industries, why did they not borrow, adapt, and utilize these productions? There must have been something vitally lacking which neither the qualities of the individual nor the stimulus of his surroundings could overcome. Some have deteriorated, others have perished; some have reached a stationary existence, while others have advanced. Through hereditary changes, nature played the game in her own way with the leading cards in her own hand, and some races lost. Hence so with races, so with individuals.

Progress Is Enhanced by the Interaction of Groups and Races.—The accumulation of civilization and the state of progress may be much determined by the interaction of races and groups. Just as individual personality is developed by contact with others, so the actions and reactions of tribes and races in contact bring into play the utility of discoveries and inventions. Thus, knowledge of any kind may by diffusion become a heritage of all races. If one tribe should acquire the art of making implements by chipping flint in a certain way, other tribes with which it comes in contact might borrow the idea and extend it, and thus it becomes spread over a wide area. However, if the original discoverer used the chipped flint for skinning animals, the one who would borrow the idea might use it to make implements of warfare.

Thus, through borrowing, progress may be a co-operative process. The reference to people in any community reveals the fact that there are few that lead and many that follow; that there is but one Edison, but there are millions that follow Edison. Even in the educational world there are few inventors and many followers. This is evidence of the large power of imitation and adaptation and of the universal habit of borrowing. On the other hand, if one chemical laboratory should discover a high explosive which may be used in blasting rock for making the foundations for buildings, a nation might borrow the idea and use it in warfare for the destruction of man.

Mr. Clark Wissler has shown in his book on *Man and Culture* that there are culture areas originating from culture centres. From these culture centres the bow-and-arrow is used over a wide area. The domestication of the horse, which occurred in central Asia, has spread over the whole world. So stone implements of culture centres have been borrowed and exchanged more or less throughout the world. The theory is that one tribe or race invented one thing because of the adaptability to good environment. The dominant necessity of a race stimulated man's inventive power, while another tribe would invent or discover some other new thing for similar reasons. But once created, not only could the products be swapped or traded, but, where this was impossible, ideas could be borrowed and adapted through imitation.

However, one should be careful not to make too hasty generalizations regarding the similar products in different parts of the world, for there is such universality of the traits of the human mind that, with similar stages of advancement and similar environments, man's adaptive power would cause him to do the same thing in very much the same way. Thus, it is possible for two races that have had no contact for a hundred thousand years to develop indigenous products of art which are very similar. To illustrate from a point of contact nearer home, it is possible for a person living in Wisconsin and one in Massachusetts, having the same general environment—physical, educational, ethnic, religious—and having the same general traits of mind, through disconnected lines of differentiation, to write two books very much alike or two magazine articles very much alike. In the question of fundamental human traits subject to the same environmental stimuli, in a general way we expect similar results.

With all this differentiation, progress as a whole represents a continuous change from primitive conditions to the present complex life, even though its line of travel leads it through the byways of differentiation. Just as the development of races has been through the process of differentiation from an early parent stock, cultural changes have followed the same law of progressive change. Just as there is a unity of the human race, there is a unity of progress that involves all mankind.

The Study of the Uncultured Races of To-Day.—It is difficult to determine the beginnings of culture and to trace its slow development. In accomplishing this, there are two main methods of procedure; the first, to find the products or remains of culture left by races now extinct, that is, of nations and peoples that have lived and flourished and passed away, leaving evidence of what they brought to the world; also, by considering what they did with the tools with which they worked, and by determining the conditions under which they lived, a general idea of their state of progress may be obtained. The second method is to determine the state of culture of living races of to-day who have been retarded or whose progress shows a case of arrested development and compare their civilization statistically observed with that of the prehistoric peoples whose state of progress exhibits in a measure similar characteristics to those of the living races.

With these two methods working together, more light is continually being thrown upon man's ancient culture. To illustrate this, if a certain kind of tool or implement is found in the culture areas of the extinct Neanderthal race and a similar tool is used by a living Australian tribe, it may be conjectured with considerable accuracy that the use of this tool was for similar purposes, and the thoughts and beliefs that clustered around its use were the same in each tribe. Thus may be estimated the degree of progress of the primitive race. Or if an inscription on a cave of an extinct race showed a similarity to an inscription used by a living race, it would seem that they had the same background for such expression, and that similar instincts, emotions, and reflections were directed to a common end. The recent study of anthropologists and archaeologists has brought to light much knowledge of primitive man which may be judged on its own evidence and own merits. The verification of these early cultures by the living races who have reached a similar degree of progress is of great importance.

The Study of Prehistoric Types.[1]—The brain capacity of modern man has changed little since the time of the Crô-Magnon race, which is the earliest ancestral type of present European races and whose existence dates back many thousand years. Possibly the weight of the brain has increased during this period because of its development, and undoubtedly its power is much greater in modern man than in this ancient type. Prior to that there are some evidences of extinct species, such as Pithecanthropus Erectus, the Grimaldi man, the Heidelberg man, and the Neanderthal. Judging from the skeletal remains that have been found of these races, there has been a general progress of cranial capacity. It is not necessary here to attempt to determine whether this has occurred from hereditary combinations or through changing environment. Undoubtedly both of these factors have been potential in increasing the brain power of man, and if we were to go farther back by way of analogy, at least, and consider the Anthropoid ape, the animal most resembling man, we find a vast contrast in his cranial capacity as compared with the lowest of the prehistoric types, or, indeed, of the lowest types of the uncultured living races.

Starting with the Anthropoid ape, who has a register of about 350 c.c., the Pithecanthropus about 900 c.c., and Neanderthal types registering as high as 1,620 c.c. of brain capacity, the best measures of the highest types of modern man show the brain capacity of 1,650 c.c. Specimens of the Crô-Magnon skulls show a brain capacity equal to that of modern man. There is a great variation in the brain capacity of the Neanderthal race as exhibited in specimens found in different centres of culture, ranging all the way from 1,296 c.c. to 1,620 c.c. Size is only one of several traits that determine brain power. Among others are the weight, convolutions, texture, and education.

A small, compact brain may have more power than a larger brain relatively lighter. Also much depends upon the centres of development. The development of the frontal area, shown by the full forehead in connection with the distance above the ear (auditory meatus), in contrast with the development of the anterior lobes is indicative of power.

It is interesting to note also that the progress of man as shown in the remnants of arts and industry corresponds in development to the development of brain capacity, showing that the physical power of man kept pace with the mental development as exhibited in his mental power displayed in the arts and industries. The discoveries in recent times of the skeletons of prehistoric man in Europe, Africa, and America, and the increased collection of implements showing cultures are throwing new light on the science of man and indicating a continuous development from very primitive beginnings.

Progress Is Indicated by the Early Cultures.—It is convenient to divide the early culture of man, based upon his development in art into the Paleolithic, or unpolished, and the Neolithic, or polished, Stone Ages.[2] The former is again divided into the Eolithic, Lower Paleolithic, and the Upper Paleolithic. In considering these divisions of relative time cultures, it must be remembered that the only way we have of measuring prehistoric time is through the geological method, based upon the Ice Ages and changes in the physical contour of the earth.

In the strata of the earth, either in the late second inter-glacial period or at the beginning of the third, chipped rocks, or eoliths, are found used by races of which the Piltdown and Heidelberg species are representatives.[3] Originally man used weapons to hammer and to cut already prepared by nature. Sharp-edged flints formed by the crushing of rocks in the descent of the glaciers or by upheavals of earth or by powerful torrents were picked up as needed for the purpose of cutting. Wherever a sharp edge was needed, these natural implements were useful. Gradually man learned to carry the best specimens with him. These he improved by chipping the edges, making them more serviceable, or chipping the eolith, so as to grasp it more easily. This represents the earliest relic of the beginning of civilization through art. Eoliths of this kind are found in Egypt in the hills bordering the Nile Valley, in Asia and America, as well as in southern Europe. Perhaps at the same period of development man selected stones suitable for crushing bones or for other purposes when hammering was necessary. These were gradually fashioned into more serviceable hammers. In the latter part of this period, known as the pre-Chellean, flint implements were considerably improved.

In the Lower Paleolithic in the pre-Neanderthal period, including what is known as the Chellean, new forms of implements are added to the earlier beginnings. Almond-shaped flint implements, followed later by long, pointed implements, indicate the future development of the stone spear, arrowhead, knife, and axe. Also smaller articles of use, such as borers, scrapers, and ploughs, appeared. The edges of all implements were rough and uneven, and the forms very imperfect.

Industrial and Social Life of Primitive Man.—In the industry of the early Neanderthal races (Acheulean) implements were increased in number and variety, being also more perfectly formed, showing the expansive art of man. At this period man was a hunter, having temporary homes in caves and shelters, which gradually became more or less permanent, and used well-fashioned implements of stone. At the close of the third interglacial period the climate was mild and moist, and mankind found the open glades suitable places for assemblages in family groups about the open fires; apparently the cooking of food and the making of implements and clothing on a small scale were the domestic occupations at this time. Hunting was the chief occupation in procuring food. The bison, the horse, the reindeer, the bear, the beaver, the wild boar had taken the place of the rhinoceros, the sabre-tooth tiger, and the elephant.

Judging from the stage of life existing at this time, and comparing this with that of the lowest living races, we may safely infer that the family associations existed at this time, even though the habitations in caves and shelters were temporary.[4]

> "Yet, when at length rude huts they first devised,
> And fires and garments; and in union sweet
> Man wedded woman, the pure joys indulged
> Of chaste connubial love, and children rose,
> The rough barbarians softened. The warm hearth
> Their frames so melted they no more could bear,

> As erst, th' uncovered skies. The nuptial bed
> Broke their wild vigor, and the fond caress
> Of prattling children from the bosom chased
> Their stern, ferocious manners."
> —LUCRETIUS, "ON THE NATURE OF THINGS."
> AFTER OSBORN.

Thus the Lower Paleolithic merged into the Upper; with the appearance of the Mousterian, Augrignacian, Solutrian, Magdalenian, and Azilian cultures followed the most advanced stage of the Neanderthal race before its final disappearance. The list of tools and implements indicates a widening scope of civilization. For war and chase and fishing, for industry and domestic life, for art, sculpture, and engraving, and for ceremonial use, a great variety of implements of stone and bone survived the life of the races.

Spears, daggers, knives, arrowheads, fish-hooks, and harpoons; hand-axes, drills, hammers, scrapers, planes, needles, pins, chisels, wedges, gravers, etchers, mortars, and pilasters; ceremonial staffs and wands—all are expressions of a fulness of industrial and social life not recognized in earlier races. Indications of religious ceremonies represent the changing mind, and the expression of mind in art suggests increased mental power.

Cultures Indicate the Mental Development of the Race.—As the art and industry to-day represent the mental processes of man, so did these primitive cultures show the inventive skill and adaptive power in the beginnings of progress. Perhaps instinct, emotion, and necessity figured more conspicuously in the early period than reflective thought, while in modern times we have more design and more planning, both in invention and construction. Also the primitive social order was more an unconscious development, and lacked purpose and directing power in comparison with present life.

But there must have been inventors and leaders in primitive times, some brains more fertile than others, that made change and progress possible. Who these unknown geniuses were human records do not indicate. In modern times we single out the superiors and call them great. The inventor, the statesman, the warrior, the king, have their achievements heralded and recorded in history. The records of achievement of the great barbarous cultures, of the Assyrians, the Egyptians, and the Hebrews, centre around some king whose tomb preserves the only records, while in reality some man unknown to us was the real author of such progress as was made. The reason is that progress was so slow that the changes passed unnoticed, being the products of many minds, each adding its increment of change. Only the king or ruler who could control the mass mind and the mass labor could make sufficient spectacular demonstration worth recording, and could direct others to build a tomb or record inscriptions to perpetuate his name.

Men of Genius Cause the Mutations Which Permit Progress.—The toiling multitudes always use the products of some inventive genius. Some individual with specialized mental traits plans something different from social usages or industrial life which changes tradition and modifies the customs and habits of the mass. Whether he be statesman, inventor, philosopher, scientist, discoverer, or military leader, he usually receives credit for the great progressive mutation which he has originated. There can be little progress without these few fertile brains, just as there could be little progress unless they were supported by the laborers who carry out the plans of the genius. While the "unknown man" is less conspicuous in the progress of the race in modern complex society, he is still a factor in all progress.

The Data of Progress.—Evolution is not necessarily progress; neither is development progress; yet the factors that enter into evolution and development are essential to progress. The laws of differentiation apply to progress as well as to evolution. In the plant and animal life everywhere this law obtains. In man it is subservient to the domination of intelligent direction, yet it is in operation all of the time. Some races are superior in certain lines, other races show superiority in other lines. Likewise, individuals exhibit differences in a similar way. Perhaps the dynamic physical or mental power of the individual or the race will not improve in itself, having reached its maximum. There is little hope that the brain of man will ever be larger or stronger, but it may become more effective through training and increased knowledge. Hence in the future we must look for achievement along co-operative and social lines. It is to social expansion and social perfection that we must look for progress in the future.

For here the accumulated power of all may be utilized in providing for the welfare of the individual, who, in turn, will by his inventive power cause humanity to progress.

The industrial, institutional, humanitarian, and educational machinery represents progress in action, but increased knowledge, higher ideals of life, broader concepts of truth, liberty of individual action which is interested in human life in its entirety, are the real indices of progress.

SUBJECTS FOR FURTHER STUDY

1. Why do some races progress and others deteriorate?

2. Compare different communities to show to what extent environment determines progress.

3. Show how the airplane is an evidence of progress. The radio. The gasoline-engine.

4. Discuss the effects of religious belief on progress.

5. Is the mental capacity of the average American greater than the average of the Greeks at the time of their highest culture?

6. What are the evidences that man will not advance in physical and mental capacity?

7. Show that the improvement of the race will be through social activity.

[1] See Chapter IV.

[2] See Chapter III.

[3] See Chapter IV.

[4] See Chapter VI.

CHAPTER III

METHODS OF RECOUNTING HUMAN PROGRESS

Difficulty of Measuring Progress.—In its larger generalization, progress may move in a straight line, but it has such a variety of expression and so many tributary causes that it is difficult to reduce it to any classification. Owing to the difficulties that attend an attempt to recite all of the details of human progress, philosophers and historians have approached the subject from various sides, each seeking to make, by means of higher generalizations, a clear course of reasoning through the labyrinth of materials. By adopting certain methods of marking off periods of existence and pointing out the landmarks of civilization, they have been able to estimate more truly the development of the race. Civilization cannot be readily measured by time; indeed, the time interval in history is of little value save to mark order and continuity. It has in itself no real significance; it is merely an arbitrary division whose importance is greatly exaggerated. But while civilization is a continuous quantity, and cannot be readily marked off into periods without destroying its movement, it is necessary to make the attempt, especially in the study of ancient or prehistoric society; for any method which groups and classifies facts in logical order is helpful to the study of human progress.

Progress May Be Measured by the Implements Used.—A very common method, based largely upon the researches of archaeologists, is to divide human society into four great periods, or ages, marked by the progress of man in the use of implements. The first of these periods is called the Stone Age, and embraces the time when man used stone for all purposes in the industrial arts so far as they had been developed. For convenience this period has been further divided into the age of ancient or unpolished implements and the age of modern or polished implements. The former includes the period when rude implements were chipped out of flint or other hard stone, without much idea of symmetry and beauty, and with no attempt to perfect or beautify them by smoothing and polishing their rough surface.

In the second period man learned to fashion more perfectly the implements, and in some instances to polish them to a high degree. Although the divisions are very general and very imperfect, they map out the great prehistoric era of man; but they must be considered as irregular, on account of the fact that the Stone Era of man occurred at different times in different tribes. Thus the inhabitants of North America were in the Stone Age less than two centuries ago, while some of the inhabitants of the South Sea Islands are in the Stone Age during the present century. It is quite remarkable that the use of stone implements was universal to all tribes and nations at some period of their existence.

After the long use of stone, man gradually became acquainted with some of the metals, and subsequently discovered the method of combining copper with tin and other alloys to form bronze, which material, to a large extent, added to the implements already in use. The Bronze Age is the most hypothetical of all these divisions, as it does not appear to have been as universal as the Stone, on account of the difficulty of obtaining metals. The use of copper by the Indians of the Lake Superior region was a very marked epoch in their development, and corresponds to the Bronze Age of other nations, although their advancement in other particulars appears to be less than that of other tribes of European origin which used bronze freely. Bronze implements have been found in great plenty in Scandinavia and Peru, and to a limited extent in North America. They certainly mark a stage of progress in advance of that of the inhabitants of the Stone Age. Bronze was the chief metal for implements throughout the early civilization of Europe.

Following the age of bronze is the Iron Age, in which the advancement of man is especially marked. The bronze implements were at first supplemented in their use by those of iron. But gradually iron implements superseded the bronze. The Iron Age still is with us. Possibly it has not yet reached its highest point. Considering the great structures built of iron, and the excessive use of iron in machinery, implements, and furniture, it is easy to realize that we are yet in this great period. Though we continue to use stone more than the ancients and more bronze for decoration and ornament than they, yet both are subordinate to the use of iron. General as the above classification is, it helps in an indefinite way to give us a central idea of progress and to mark off, somewhat indefinitely, periods of development.

The Development of Art.—Utility was the great purpose underlying the foundation of the industrial arts. The stone axe, or celt, was first made for a distinct service, but, in order to perfect its usefulness, its lines became more perfect and its surface more highly polished. So we might say for the spear-head, the knife, or the olla. Artistic lines and decorative beauty always followed the purpose of use. This could be applied to all of the products of man's invention to transform parts of nature to his use. On account of the durability of form, the attempt to trace the course of civilization by means of the development of the fine arts has met with much success. Though the idea of beauty is not essential to the preservation of man or to the making of the state, it has exerted a great influence in individual-building and in society-building. In our higher emotional natures aesthetic ideas have ruled with imperial sway.

But primitive ideas of beauty appear to us very crude, and even repulsive. The adornment of person with bright though rudely colored garments, the free use of paint on the person, and the promiscuous use of jewelry, as practised by the primitive peoples, present a great contrast to modern usage. Yet it is easy to trace the changes in custom and, moreover, to determine the origin of present customs. So also in representative art, the rude sketch of an elephant or a buffalo on ivory or stone and the finished picture by a Raphael are widely separated in genius and execution, but there is a logical connection between the two found in the slowly evolving human activities. The rude figure of a god moulded roughly from clay and the lifelike model by an Angelo have the same relations to man in his different states. The same comparison may be made between the low, monotonous moaning of the savage and the rapturous music of a Patti, or between the beating of the tom-tom and the lofty strains of a Mozart.

Progress Is Estimated by Economic Stages.—The progress of man is more clearly represented by the successive economic stages of his life. Thus we have first the *primal nomadic* period, in which man was a wanderer, subsisting on roots and berries, and with no definite social organization. This period, like all primary periods, is largely hypothetical. Having learned to capture game and fish, he entered what might be called the *fisher-hunter* stage, although he was still a nomad, and rapidly spread over a large part of the earth's surface, wandering from forest to forest and from stream to stream, searching for the means of subsistence and clothing.

When man learned to domesticate animals he made a great step forward and entered what is known as the *pastoral* period, in which his chief occupation was the care of flocks and herds. This contributed much to his material support and quickened his social and intellectual movement. After a time, when he remained in one place a sufficient time to harvest a short crop, he began agriculture in a tentative way, while his chief concern was yet with flocks and herds. He soon became permanently settled, and learned more fully the art of agriculture, and then entered the permanent *agricultural* stage. It was during this period that he made the most rapid advances in the industrial arts and in social order. This led to more densely populated communities, with permanent homes and the necessary development of law and government.

As the products of industry increased men began to exchange "the relatively superfluous for the relatively necessary," and trade in the form of barter became a permanent custom. This led to the use of money and a more extended system of exchange, and man entered the *commercial* era. This gave him a wider intercourse with surrounding tribes and nations, and brought about a greater diversity of ideas. The excessive demand for exchangeable goods, the accumulation of wealth, and the enlarged capacity for enjoyment centred the activities of life in industry, and man entered the *industrial* stage. At first he employed hand power for manufacturing goods, but soon he changed to power manufacture, brought about by discovery and invention. Water and steam were now applied to turn machinery, and the new conditions of production changed the whole industrial life. A revolution in industrial society caused an immediate shifting of social life. Classes of laborers in the great industrial army became prominent, and production was carried on in a gigantic way. We are still in this industrial world, and as electricity comes to the aid of steam we may be prepared for even greater changes in the future than we have witnessed in the past.[1]

In thus presenting the course of civilization by the different periods of economic life, we must keep the mind free from conventional ideas. For, while the general course of economic progress is well indicated, there was a slow blending of each period into the succeeding one. There is no formal procedure in the progress of man. Yet we might infer from the way in which some writers present this matter that society moved forward in regular order, column after column. From the formal and forcible way in which they have presented the history of early society, one might imagine that a certain tribe, having become weary of tending cattle and goats, resolved one fine morning to change from the pastoral life to agriculture, and that all of the tribes on earth immediately concluded to do the same, when, in truth, the change was slow and gradual, while the centuries passed away.

It is well to consider that in the expanded industrial life of man the old was not replaced, but supplemented, by the new, and that after the pastoral stage was entered, man continued to hunt and fish, and that after formal agriculture was begun the tending of flocks and herds continued, and fishing was practised at intervals. But each succeeding occupation became for the time the predominant one, while others were relatively subordinate. Even to-day, while we have been rushing forward in recent years at a rapid rate, under the power of steam and electricity, agriculture and commerce have made marvellous improvement. Though we gain the new, nothing of the old is lost. The use of flocks and herds, as well as fish and game, increases each year, although not relatively.

Progress Is Through the Food Supply.—This is only another view of the economic life. The first period is called the natural subsistence period, when man used such food as he found prepared for him by nature. It corresponds to the primal nomadic period of the last classification. From this state he advanced to the use of fish for food, and then entered the third period, when native grains were obtained through a limited cultivation of the soil. After this followed a period in which meat and milk were the chief articles of food. Finally the period of extended and permanent agriculture was reached, and farinaceous food by cultivation became the main support of life. The significance of this classification is observed in the fact that the amount, variety, and quality of the food available determine the possibility of man's material and spiritual advancement. As the food supply lies at the foundation of human existence, prosperity is measured to a large extent by the food products. The character of the food affects to a great extent the mental and moral capabilities of man; that is, it limits the possibilities of civilization. Even in modern civilization the effect of poor food on intellect, morals, and social order is easily observed.

Progress Is Estimated by Different Forms of Social Order.—It is only a more general way of estimating political life, and perhaps a broader way, for it includes the entire social development. By this classification man is first represented as wandering in a solitary state with the smallest amount of association with his fellows necessary to his existence and perpetuation, and with no social organization. This status of man is hypothetical, and gives only a starting point for the philosophy of higher development. No savage tribes have yet been discovered in which there was not at least association of individuals in groups, although organization might not yet have appeared. It is true that some of the lower tribes, like the Fuegians of South America, have very tentative forms of social and political association. They wander in loosely constructed groups, which constantly shift in association, being without permanent organization. Yet the purely solitary man is merely conjectural.

It is common for writers to make a classification of social groups into primary and secondary.[2] The primary social groups are: first, the family based upon biological relations, supported by the habit of association; second, the play group of children, in which primitive characters of social order appear, and a third group is the association of adults in a neighborhood meeting. In the formation of these groups, the process of social selection is always in evidence. Impulse, feeling, and emotion play the greater parts in the formation of these primitive groups, while choice based on rational selection seldom appears.

The secondary groups are those which originate through the differentiation of social functions in which the contact of individuals is less intimate than in the primary group. Such voluntary associations as a church, labor organization, or scientific society may be classified as secondary in time and in importance.

Next above the human horde is represented the forced association of men in groups, each group struggling for its own existence. Within the group there was little protection and little social order, although there was more or less authority of leadership manifested. This state finally led to the establishment of rudimentary forms of government, based upon blood relationship. These groups enlarged to full national life. This third stage finally passed to the larger idea of international usage, and is prospective of a world state. These four stages of human society, so sweeping in their generalization, still point to the idea of the slow evolution of social order.

The Development of Family Life.—Starting with the hypothesis that man at one time associated in a state of promiscuity, he passed through the separate stages of polyandry and polygamy, and finally reached a state of monogamy and the pure home life of to-day. Those who have advocated this doctrine have failed to substantiate it clearly so as to receive from scholars the recognition of authority. All these forms of family life except the first have been observed among the savage tribes of modern life, but there are not sufficient data to prove that the human race, in the order of its development, must have passed through these four stages. However, it is true that the modern form of marriage and pure home life did not always exist, but are among the achievements of modern civilization. There certainly has been a gradual improvement in the relations of the members of the household, and notwithstanding the defects of faithlessness and ignorance, the modern family is the social unit and the hope of modern social progress.

The Growth of Political Life.—Many have seen in this the only true measure of progress, for it is affirmed that advancement in civil life is the essential element of civilization. Its importance in determining social order makes it a central factor in all progress. The *primitive family* represents the germ of early political foundation. It was the first organized unit of society, and contained all of the rudimentary forms of government. The executive, the judicial, the legislative, and the administrative functions of government were all combined in one simple family organization. The head of the family was king, lord, judge, priest, and military commander all in one. As the family expanded it formed the *gens* or *clan,* with an enlarged family life and more systematic family government. The religious life expanded also, and a common altar and a common worship were instituted.

A slight progress toward social order and the tendency to distribute the powers of government are to be observed. Certain property was held in common and certain laws regulated the family life. The family groups continued to enlarge by natural increase and by adoption, all those coming into the gens submitting to its laws, customs, and social usage. Finally several gentes united into a brotherhood association called by the Greeks a *phratry*, by the Romans a *curia*. This brotherhood was organized on a common religious basis, with a common deity and a central place of worship. It also was used partially as the basis of military organization. This group represents the first unit based upon locality. From it spring the ward idea and the idea of local self-government.

The *tribe* represented a number of gentes united for religious and military purposes. Although its principal power was military, there were a common altar and a common worship for all members of the tribe. The chief, or head of the tribe, was the military leader, and usually performed an important part in all the affairs of the tribe. As the tribe became the seat of power for military operations, the gens remained as the foundation of political government, for it was the various heads of the gentes who formed the council of the chief or king and later laid the foundation of the senate, wherever instituted. It was common for the tribe in most instances to pass into a village community before developing full national life. There were exceptions to this, where tribes have passed directly into well-organized groups without the formation of the village or the city.

The *village community*, next in logical order, represents a group of closely related people located on a given territory, with a half-communal system of government. There were the little group of houses forming the village proper and representing the different homes of the family group. There were the common pasture-land, the common woodland, and the fertile fields for cultivation. These were all owned, except perhaps the house lot, by the entire community, and every year the tillable land was parcelled out by the elders of the community to the heads of families for tillage. Usually the tiller of the soil had a right to the crop, although among the early Greeks the custom seems to be reversed, and the individual owned the land, but was compelled to place its proceeds into a common granary. The village community represents the transition from a nomadic to a permanent form of government, and was common to all of the Aryan tribes. The federation of the village communities or the expansion of the tribes formed the Greek city-state, common to all of the Greek communities. It represents the real beginning of civic life among the nations.

The old family organization continued to exist, although from this time on there was a gradual separation of the functions of government. The executive, legislative, and judicial processes became more clearly defined, and special duties were assigned to officers chosen for a particular purpose. Formal law, too, appeared as the expression of the will of a definitely organized community. Government grew more systematic, and expanded into a well-organized municipality. There was less separation of the duties of officers than now, but there was a constant tendency for government to unfold and for each officer to have his specific powers and duties defined. A deity watched over the city, and a common shrine for worship was set up for all members of the municipality.

The next attempt to enlarge government was by federation and by conquest and domination.[3] The city of Rome represents, first, a federation of tribal city groups, and, finally, the dominant city ruling over many other cities and much territory. From this it was only a step to the empire and imperial sway. Athens in her most prosperous period attempted to do the same, but was not entirely successful. After the decline of the Roman power there arose from the ruins of the fallen empire the modern nationalities, which used all forms of government hitherto known. They partook of democracy, aristocracy, or imperialism, and even attempted, in some instances, to combine the principles of all three in one government. While the modern state developed some new characteristics, it included the elements of the Greek and Roman governments. The relations of these new states developed a new code of law, based upon international relations. Though treaties were made between the Greeks and the Romans in their first international relations, and much earlier between the Hebrews and the Phoenicians, international law is of practically modern origin. At present modern nations have an extended and intricate code of laws governing their relations. It is an extension of government beyond the boundaries of nationality.

Through commerce, trade, and political intercourse the nations of the Western World are drawn more closely together, and men talk of a world citizenship. A wide philanthropy, rapid and cheap transportation, the accompanying influences of travel, and a world market for the products of the earth, all tend to level the barriers of nationality and to develop universal citizenship. The prophets of our day talk of the coming world state, which is not likely to appear so long as the barriers of sea and mountain remain; yet each year witnesses a closer blending of the commercial, industrial, and political interests of all nations. Thus we see how governments have been evolved and national life expanded in accordance with slowly developing civilization. Although good government and a high state of civilization are not wholly in the relation of cause and effect, they always accompany each other, and the progress of man may be readily estimated from the standpoint of the development of political institutions and political life.

Religion Important in Civilization.—It is not easy to trace the development of man by a consideration of the various religious beliefs entertained at different periods of his existence. Yet there is unmistakably a line of constant development to be observed in religion, and as a rule its progress is an index of the improvement of the race. No one can contrast the religion of the ancient nations with the modern Christian religion without being impressed with the vast difference in conception and in practice existing between them. In the early period of barbarism, and even of savagery, religious belief was an important factor in the development of human society.

It is no less important to-day, and he who recounts civilization without giving it a prominent place has failed to obtain a comprehensive view of the philosophy of human development. From the family altar of the Greeks to the state religion; from the rude altar of Abraham in the wilderness to the magnificent temple of Solomon at Jerusalem; from the harsh and cruel tenets of the Oriental religions to the spiritual conception and ethical practice of the Christian religion, one observes a marked progress. We need only go to the crude unorganized superstition of the savage or to the church of the Middle Ages to learn that the power and influence of religion is great in human society building.

The Progress Through Moral Evolution.—The moral development of the race, although more difficult to determine than the intellectual, may prove an index to the progress of man. The first formal expression of moral practice is the so-called race morality or group morality, based upon mutual aid for common defense. This is found to-day in all organized groups, such as the boy gang, the Christian church, the political party, the social set, the educational institution, and, indeed, the state itself; but wherever found it has its source in a very primitive group action. In the primitive struggle for existence man had little sympathy for his fellows, the altruistic sentiment being very feeble. But gradually through the influence of the family life sympathy widened and deepened in its onward flow until, joining with the group morality, it entered the larger world of ethical practice.

This phase of moral culture had its foundation in the sympathy felt by the mother for her offspring, a sympathy that gradually extended to the immediate members of the household. As the family expanded into the state, human sympathy expanded likewise, until it became national in its significance. Through this process there finally came a world-wide philanthropy which recognizes the sufferings of all human beings. This sympathy has been rapidly increased by the culture of the intellect, the higher development of the sensibilities, and the refinement of the emotions; thus along the track of altruism or ethical development, which had its foundation in primitive life, with its ever widening and enlarging circles, the advancement of humanity may be traced. The old egoism, the savage warfare for existence, has been constantly tempered by altruism, which has been a saving quality in the human race.

Intellectual Development of Man.—Some philosophers have succeeded in recounting human progress by tracing the intellectual development of the race. This is possible, for everything of value that has been done, and which has left a record, bears the mark of man's intellect. In the early period of his existence, man had sufficient intellect to direct his efforts to satisfy the common wants of life. This exercise of the intellectual faculty has accompanied man's every movement, but it is best observed in the products of his industry and the practice of social order. By doing and making, the intellect grows, and it is only by observing the phenomena of active life that we get a hint or trace of the powers and capacities of the mind. But after man begins the process of reflective thinking, his intellectual activities become stronger, and it is much easier to trace his development by considering the condition of religion, law, philosophy, literature, sculpture, art, and architecture. These represent the best products of the mind, and it is along this intellectual highway that the best results of civilization are found. During the modern period of progressive life systematic education has forced the intellectual faculties through a more rapid course, giving predominance to intellectual life everywhere. The intellectual development of nations or the intellectual development of man in general is a theme of never-tiring interest, as it represents his noblest achievements.

Man from the very beginning has had a desire for knowledge, to satisfy curiosity. Gradually, however, he had a desire to know in order to increase utility, and finally he reaches the highest state of progress in desiring to know for the sake of knowing. Thus he proceeds from mere animal curiosity to the idealistic state of discovering "truth for truth's sake." These are qualities not only of the individual in his development but of the racial group and, indeed, in a larger way of all mankind; intelligence developed in the attempt of man to discover the nature of the results of his instinctive, impulsive, or emotional actions. Later he sought causes of these results. Here we have involved increased knowledge as a basis of human action and the use of that knowledge through discriminating intelligence. The intellect thus represents the selective and directive process in the use of knowledge. Hence, intelligent behavior of the individual or of the group comes only after accumulated knowledge based on experience. The process of trial and error thus gives rise to reflective thinking. It is a superior use of the intellect that more than anything else distinguishes the adult from the child or modern man from the primitive.

Change from Savagery to Barbarism.—Perhaps one of the broadest classifications of ancient society, based upon general characteristics of progress, makes the two general divisions of savagery and barbarism, and subdivides each of these into three groups. The lowest status of savagery represents man as little above the brute creation, subsisting upon roots and berries, and with no knowledge of art or of social order. The second period, called the middle status of savagery, represents man using fire, and using fish for food, and having corresponding advancement in other ways. The upper status of savagery begins with the use of the bow-and-arrow and extends to the period of the manufacture and use of pottery.

At this point the period of barbarism begins. Its lower status, beginning with the manufacture of pottery, extends to the time of the domestication of animals. The middle status includes not only the domestication of animals in the East but the practice of irrigation in the West and the building of walls from stone and adobe brick. The upper status is marked by the use of iron and extends to the introduction of the phonetic alphabet and literary composition. At this juncture civilization is said to dawn.

"Commencing," says Mr. Morgan, the author of this classification, in his *Ancient Society*, "with the Australians and the Polynesians, following with the American Indian tribes, and concluding with the Roman and Grecian, which afford the best exemplification of the six great stages of human progress, the sum of their united experiences may be supposed to fairly represent that of the human family from the middle status of savagery to the end of the ancient civilization." By this classification the Australians would be placed in the middle status of savagery, and the early Greeks and Romans in the upper status of barbarism, while the Pueblo Indians of New Mexico would be placed in the middle status of barbarism. This is an excellent system for estimating the progress of ancient society, for around these initial periods may be clustered all of the elements of civilization. It is of especial value in the comparative study of different races and tribes.

Civilization Includes All Kinds of Human Progress.—The above representation of the principal methods of recounting civilization shows the various phases of human progress. Although each one is helpful in determining the progress of man from a particular point of view, none is sufficient to marshal all of the qualities of civilization in a completed order. For the entire field of civilization should include all the elements of progress, and this great subject must be viewed from every side before it can be fairly represented to the mind of the student. The true nature of civilization has been more clearly presented in thus briefly enumerating the different methods of estimating human progress. But we must remember that civilization, though continuous, is not uniform. The qualities of progress which are strong in one tribe or nation are weak in others. It is the total of the characteristics of man and the products of his activity that represents his true progress. Nations have arisen, developed, and passed away; tribes have been swept from the face of the earth before a complete development was possible; and races have been obliterated by the onward march of civilization. But the best products of all nations have been preserved for the service of others. Ancient Chaldea received help from central Asia; Egypt and Judea from Babylon; Greece from Egypt; Rome from Greece; and all Europe and America have profited from the culture of Greece and Rome and the religion of Judea. There may be a natural growth, maturity, and decay of nations, but civilization moves ever on toward a higher and more diversified life. The products of human endeavor arrange themselves on the side of man in his attempt to master himself and nature.

TABLE SHOWING METHODS OF RECOUNTING HUMAN PROGRESS

I. Method of the Kind of Implements Used.

    1. Paleolithic, or Old Stone, Age.
    2. Neolithic, or New Stone, Age.
    3. Incidental use of copper, tin, and other metals.
    4. The making of pottery.
    5. The age of bronze.
    6. The iron age.

II. Method by Art Development.

    1. Primitive drawings in caves and engraving on ivory and wood.
    2. The use of color in decoration of objects, especially in decoration of the body.
    3. Beginnings of sculpture and carving figures, animals, gods, and men.
    4. Pictorial representations--the pictograph.
    5. Representative art in landscapes.
    6. Perspective drawing.
    7. Idealistic art.
    8. Industrial arts.

III. Method of Economic Stages.

    1. The Nomadic Stage.
    2. The Hunter-Fisher Stage.
    3. The Pastoral Period.
    4. The Agricultural Period.
    5. The Commercial Period.
    6. The Period of Industrial Organization.

IV. Progress Estimated by the Food Supply.

    1. Natural subsistence Period.
    2. Fish and shell fish.
    3. Cultivation of native grains.
    4. Meat and milk.
    5. Farinaceous foods by systematic agriculture.

V. Method of Social Order.

    1. Solitary state of man (hypothetical).
    2. The human horde.
    3. Small groups for purposes of association.
    4. The secret society.
    5. The religious cult.
    6. Closely integrated groups for defense.
    7. Amalgamated or federated groups.
    8. The Race.

VI. The Family Development.

    1. State of promiscuity (hypothetical).
    2. Polyandry.
    3. Polygamy.
    4. Patriarchal family with polygamy.
    5. The Monogamic family.

VII. Progress Measured by Political Organization.

      1. The organized horde about religious ideas.

      2. The completed family organization.
          a. Family.
          b. Gens.
          c. The Phratry.
          d. Patriarchal family.
          e. Tribe.
      3. The Ethnic state.
      4. State formed by conflict and amalgamation.
      5. International relations.
      6. The World State (Idealistic).

VIII. Religious Development.

      1. Belief in spiritual beings.
      2. Recognition of the spirit of man and other spirits.
      3. Animism.
      4. Anthropomorphic religion.
      5. Spiritual concept of religion.
      6. Ethnical religions.
      7. Forms of religious worship and religious practice.

IX. Moral Evolution.

      1. Race morality (gang morality).
      2. Sympathy for fellow beings.
      3. Sympathy through blood relationship.
      4. Patriotism: love of race and country.
      5. World Ethics.

X. Progress Through Intellectual Development.

      1. Sensation and reflex action.
      2. Instinct and emotion.
      3. Impulse and adaptability.
      4. Reflective thought.
      5. Invention and discovery.
      6. Rational direction of human life.
      7. Philosophy.
      8. Science.

XI. Progress Through Savagery and Barbarism.

      1. Lower status of savagery.
      2. Middle status of savagery.
      3. Upper status of savagery.
      4. Lower status of barbarism.
      5. Middle status of barbarism.
      6. Upper status of barbarism.
      7. Civilization (?).

SUBJECTS FOR FURTHER STUDY

1. In what other ways than those named in this chapter may we estimate the progress of man?

2. Discuss the evidences of man's mental and spiritual progress.

3. The relation of wealth to progress.

4. The relation of the size of population to the prosperity of a nation.

5. Enumerate the arguments that the next destructive war will destroy civilization.

6. In what ways do you think man is better off than he was one hundred years ago? One thousand years ago?

7. In what ways did the suffering caused by the Great War indicate an increase in world ethics?

[1] See Chapter XXVII.

[2] See Cooley, *Social Organization*, chap. III.

[3] The transition from the ethnic state to the modern civic state was through conflict, conquest, and race amalgamation.

FIRST STEPS OF PROGRESS

CHAPTER IV

PREHISTORIC MAN

The Origin of Man Has not Yet Been Determined.—Man's origin is still shrouded in mystery, notwithstanding the accumulated knowledge of the results of scientific investigation in the field and in the laboratory. The earliest historical records and relics of the seats of ancient civilization all point backward to an earlier period of human life. Looking back from the earliest civilizations along the Euphrates and the Nile that have recorded the deeds of man so that their evidences could be handed down from generation to generation, the earlier prehistoric records of man stretch away in the dim past for more than a hundred thousand years. The time that has elapsed from the earliest historical records to the present is only a few minutes compared to the centuries that preceded it.

Wherever we go in the field of knowledge, we shall find evidences of man's great antiquity. We know at least that he has been on earth a long, long period. As to the method of his appearance, there is no absolutely determining evidence. Yet science has run back into the field of conjecture with such strong lines that we may assume with practical certainty something of his early life. He stands at the head of the zoological division of the animal kingdom. The Anthropoid Ape is the animal that most nearly resembles man. It might be said to stand next to man in the procession of species. So far as our knowledge can ascertain, it appears that man was developed in the same manner as the higher types in the animal and vegetable world, namely, by the process of evolution, and by evolution we mean continuous progressive change according to law, from external and internal stimuli. The process of evolution is not a process of creation, nor does evolution move in a straight line, but through the process of differentiation. In no other way can one account for the multitudes of the types and races of the human being, except by this process of differentiation which is one of the main factors of evolution. Accompanying the process of differentiation is that of specialization and integration. When types become highly specialized they fail to adapt themselves to new environments, and other types not so highly specialized prevail. So far as the human race is concerned, it seems to be evolved according to the law of sympodial development—that is, a certain specialized part of the human race develops certain traits and is limited in its adaptability to a specific environment. Closely allied with this are some individuals or groups possessing human traits that are less highly specialized, and hence are adaptable to new conditions. Under new conditions the main stem of development perishes and the budded branch survives.

We have abundant pictures of this in prehistoric times, and records show that this also has been the common lot of man. Modern man thus could not have been developed from any of the living species of the Anthropoid Apes, but he might have had a common origin in the physical, chemical, and vital forces that produced the apes. One line of specialization made the ape, another line made man. Subsequently the separation of man into the various races and species came about by the survival of some races for a time, and then to be superseded by a branch of the same race which differentiated in a period of development before high specialization had taken place.

Methods of Recounting Prehistoric Time.[1]—Present time is measured in terms of centuries, years, months, weeks, days, hours, minutes, and seconds, but the second is the determining power of mechanical measurement, though it is derived mainly by the movement of the earth around the sun and the turning of the earth on its axis. Mechanically we have derived the second as the unit. It is easy for us to think in hours or days or weeks, though it may be the seconds tick off unnoticed and the years glide by unnoticed; but it is difficult to think in centuries—more difficult in millions of years. The little time that man has been on earth compared with the creation of the earth makes it difficult for us to estimate the time of creation. The much less time in the historical period makes it seem but a flash in the movement of the creation.

TWENTY-FOUR-HOUR DIAL ILLUSTRATING HUMAN CHRONOLOGY[2]

Twenty-five thousand years equals one hour

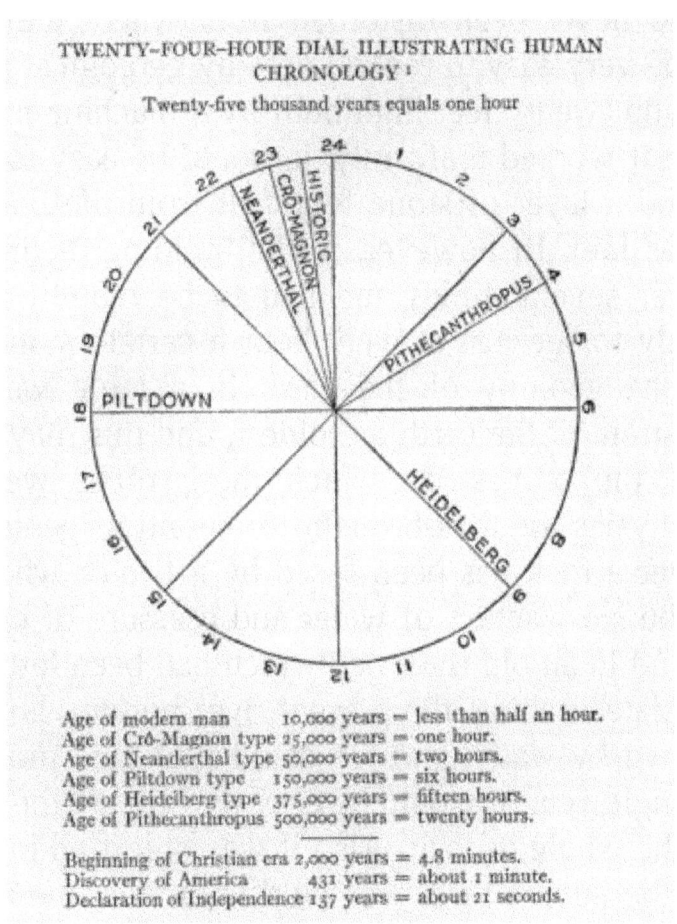

Twenty-four hour dial

```
Age of modern man         10,000 years  = less than half an hour.
Age of Crô-Magnon type    25,000 years  = one hour.
Age of Neanderthal type   50,000 years  = two hours.
Age of Piltdown type      150,000 years = six hours.
Age of Heidelberg type    375,000 years = fifteen hours.
Age of Pithecanthropus    500,000 years = twenty hours.
```

```
Beginning of Christian era    2,000 years = 4.8 minutes.
Discovery of America            431 years = about 1 minute.
Declaration of Independence     137 years = about 21 seconds.
```

There are four main methods of determining prehistoric time.[3] One is called the (1) *geologic method*, which is based upon the fact that, in a slowly cooling earth and the action of water and frost, cold and heat, storm and glacier and volcanic eruption, the rocks on the earth are of different ages. If they had never been disturbed from where they were first laid down, it would be very easy to reckon time by geological processes. If you had a stone column twenty feet high built by a machine in ten hours' time, and granting that it worked uniformly, it would be easy to see just at what hour of the period a layer of stone four feet from the bottom, or ten feet from the top, was laid. If, however, in the building of the wall, it should have toppled over several times and had to be rebuilt, it would require considerable study to see just at what hour a certain stone was put in the wall. Studying the geology of the earth in a large way, it is easy to determine what strata of the earth are oldest, and this may be verified by a consideration of the process in which these rocks were being made. Chemistry and physics are thus brought to the aid of geology. It is easy to determine whether a rock has been fused by a fire or whether it has been constructed by the slow action of water and pressure of other rocks. If to-day we should find in an old river bed which had been left high and dry on a little mesa or plateau above the present river bottom, layers of earth that had been put down by water, and we could find how much of each layer was made in a single year, it would be easy to estimate the number of years it took to make the whole deposit. Also if we could find in the lowest layer certain relics of the human race, we could know that the race lived at that time. If we should find relics later on of a different nature, we should be able to estimate the progress of civilization.

The second method is of (2) *paleontology*, which is developed along with geology. In this we have both the vertebrate and invertebrate paleontology, which are divisions of the science which treats of ancient forms of animal and vegetable life. There are many other divisions of paleontology, some devoting themselves entirely to animal life and others to vegetable, as, for instance, paleobotany. As plants and animals have gradually developed from lower to higher forms and the earth has been built gradually by formations at different periods of existence, by a comparison of the former development with the latter, that is, comparison with the earth, or inorganic, development to the life, or organic, development, we are enabled to get a comparative view of duration. Thus, if in a layer of earth, geological time is established and there should be found bones of an animal, the bones of a man, and fossilized forms of ancient plants, it would be easy to determine their relative ages.

The third method is that of (3) *anatomy*, which is a study of the comparative size and shape of the bones of man and other animals as a method of showing relative periods of existence. Also, just as the structure of the bones of a child, as compared with that of a man, would determine their relative ages, so the bones of the species that have been preserved through fossilization may show the relative ages of different types of animals. The study of the skeletons of animals, including those of man, has led to the science of anthropometry.

The fourth method is to study the procession of man by (4) *cultures*, or the industrial and ornamental implements that have been preserved in the river drift, rocks, and caves of the earth from the time that man used them until they were discovered. Just as we have to-day models of the improvement of the sewing-machine, the reaper, or the flying-machine, each one a little more perfect, so we shall find in the relics of prehistoric times this same gradual development—first a stone in its natural state used for cutting, then chipped to make it more perfect, and finally beautified in form and perfected by polishing.

Thus we shall find progress from the natural stone boulder used for throwing and hammering, the developed product made by chipping and polishing the natural boulder, making it more useful and more beautiful, and so for all the multitude of implements used in the hunt and in domestic affairs. Not only do we have here an illustration of continuous progress in invention and use, but also an adaptation of new material, for we pass from the use of stone to that of metals, probably in the prehistoric period, although the beginnings of the use of bronze and iron come mainly within the periods of historical records.

It is not possible here to follow the interesting history of the glacial movement, but a few words of explanation seem necessary. The Ice Age, or the glacial period, refers to a span of time ranging from 500,000 years ago, at the beginning of the first glaciation, to the close of the post-glacial period, about 25,000 years ago. During this period great ice caps, ranging in the valleys and spreading out on the plains over a broad area, proceeded from the north of Europe to the south, covering at the extreme stages nearly the entire surface of the continent. This great movement consists of four distinct forward movements and their return movements. There is evidence to show that before the south movement of the first great ice cap, a temperate climate extended very far toward the pole and gave opportunity for vegetation now extinct in that region.

But as the river of ice proceeded south, plants and animals retreated before it, some of them changing their nature to endure the excessive cold. Then came a climatic change which melted the ice and gradually drove the margin of the glacier farther north. Immediately under the influence of the warm winds the vegetation and animals followed slowly at a distance the movement of the glacier. Then followed a long inter-glacial period before the southerly movement of the returning ice cap. This in turn retreated to the north, and thus four separate times this great movement, one of the greatest geological phenomena of the earth, occurred, leaving an opportunity to study four different glacial periods with three warmer interglacial and one warm post-glacial.

This movement gave great opportunity for the study of geology, paleontology, and the archeology of man. That is, the story of the relationship of the earth to plant, animal, and man was revealed. The regularity of these movements and the amount of material evidence found furnish a great opportunity for measuring geological time movements and hence the life of plants and animals, including man.

The table on page 64 will contribute to the clearness of this brief statement about the glacial periods.

THE ICE AGE IN EUROPE[5]

Geological time-unit 25,000 years

	GLACIERS	RELATIVE TIME UNIT	TIME YRS.	TOTAL TIME YRS.	HUMAN LIFE	ANIMAL AND PLANT LIFE
	Post-Glacial Daum Geschintz Bühl	1	25,000	25,000	Crô-Magnon Azilian Magdalenian Solutrian Aurignacian	Horse, Stag, Reindeer, Musk-Ox, Arctic Fox, Pine, Birch, Oak
	4th Glacial Wurm Ice	1	25,000	50,000	Mousterian Neanderthal	Reindeer, period of Tundra, Alpine, Steppe, Meadow
Q U A T E R N A R Y	3d Interglacial	4	100,000	150,000	Pre-Neanderthal Piltdown	Last warm Asiatic and African animals
	3d Glacial Riss	1	25,000	175,000		Woolly Mammoth, Rhinoceros, Reindeer
	2d Interglacial Mindel-Riss	8	200,000	375,000	Heidelberg Race	African and Asiatic Animals, Elephant, Hippopotamus
	2d Glacial Mindel	1	25,000	400,000		Cold weather animals
	1st Interglacial	3	75,000	475,000	Pithecanthropus Erectus	Hippopotamus, Elephant, African and Asiatic plants
	1st Glacial	1	25,000	500,000		
T E R T I A R Y						

Prehistoric Types of the Human Race.—The earliest record of human life yet discovered is the *Pithecanthropus Erectus* (Trinil), the apelike man who walked upright, found in Java by Du Bois, about the year 1892. Enough of the skeletal remains of human beings were found at this time to indicate a man of rather crude form and low brain capacity (about 885 c.c.), with possible powers of speech but with no probably developed language or no assumption of the acquaintance with the arts of life.[4]

The remains of this man associated with the remains of one other skeleton, probably a woman, and with the bones of extinct animals, were found in a geological stratum which indicates his age at about 500,000 years. Professor McGregor, after a careful anatomical study, has reproduced the head and bust of Pithecanthropus, which helps us to visualize this primitive species as of rather low cultural type. The low forehead, massive jaw, and receding chin give us a vision of an undeveloped species of the human race, in some respects not much above the anthropoid apes, yet in other characters distinctly human.

There follows a long interval of human development which is only conjectural until the discovery of the bones of the Heidelberg man, found at the south of the River Neckar. These are the first records of the human race found in southern Europe. The type of man is still apelike in some respects, but far in advance of the Pithecanthropus in structure and general appearance. The restoration by the Belgian artist Mascré under the direction of Professor A. Rotot, of Brussels, is indicative of larger brain capacity than the Trinil race. It had a massive jaw, distinctive nose, heavy arched brows, and still the receding chin. Not many cultural remains were found in strata of the second interglacial period along with the remains of extinct animals, such as the ancient elephant, Etruscan rhinoceros, primitive bison, primitive ox, Auvergne bear, and lion. A fauna and a flora as well as a geological structure were found which would indicate that this race existed at this place about 375,000 years ago. From these evidences very little may be determined of the Heidelberg man's cultural development, but much may be inferred. Undoubtedly, like the Pithecanthropus, he was a man without the tools of civilization, or at least had not developed far in this way.

About 150,000 years ago there appeared in Europe races of mankind that left more relics of their civilization.[6] These were the Neanderthaloid races. There is no evidence of the connection of these races with the Java man or the Heidelberg man. Here, as elsewhere in the evolution of races and species, nature does not work in a straight line of descent, but by differentiation and variation.

In 1856 the first discovery of a specimen of the Neanderthal man was found at the entrance of a small ravine on the right bank of the River Dussel, in Rhenish Prussia. This was the first discovery of the Paleolithic man to cause serious reflection on the possibility of a prehistoric race in Europe. Its age is estimated at 50,000 years. This was followed by other discoveries of the Mid-Pleistocene period, until there were a number of discoveries of similar specimens of the Neanderthal race, varying in some respects from each other. The first had a brain capacity of 1230 c.c., while that of the average European is about 1500 c.c. Some of the specimens showed a skull capacity larger than the first specimen, but the average is lower than that of any living race, unless it be that of the Australians.

Later were discovered human remains of a somewhat higher type, known as the Aurignacian, of the Crô-Magnon race. These are probably ancestors of the living races of Europe existing 25,000 to 50,000 years ago. They represent the first races to which may be accorded definite relationship with the recent races.

Thus we have evidences of the great antiquity of man and a series of remains showing continual advancement over a period of nearly 500,000 years—the Pithecanthropus, Heidelberg, Piltdown, and Neanderthal, though expressing gradations of development in the order named, appear to be unrelated in their origin and descent, and are classed as separate species long since extinct. The Crô-Magnon people seem more directly related to modern man. Perhaps in the Neolithic Age they may have been the forebears of present races, either through direct or indirect lines.

The Unity of the Human Race.—Though there are evidences, as shown above, that there were many branches of the human race, or species, some of which became extinct without leaving any records of the passing on of their cultures to others, there is a pretty generally concerted opinion that all branches of the human race are related and have sprung from the same ancestors. There have been differences of opinion regarding this view, some holding that there are several centres of development in which the precursor of man assumed a human form (polygenesis), and others holding that according to the law of differentiation and zoological development there must have been at some time one origin of the species (monogenesis). So far as the scientific investigation of mankind is concerned, it is rather immaterial which theory is accepted. We know that multitudes of tribes and races differ in minor parts of structure, differ in mental capacity, and hence in qualities of civilization, and yet in general form, brain structure, and mental processes, it is the same human being wherever found. So we may assume that there is a unity of the race.

If we consider the human race to have sprung from a single pair, or even the development of man from a single species, it must have taken a long time to have developed the great marks of racial differences that now exist. The question of unity or plurality of race origins has been much discussed, and is still somewhat in controversy, although the predominance of evidence is much in favor of the descent of man from a single species and from a single place. The elder Agassiz held that there were several separate species of the race, which accounts for the wide divergence of characteristics and conditions. But it is generally admitted from a zoological standpoint that man originated from a single species, although it does not necessarily follow that he came from a single pair. It is the diversity or the unity of the race from a single pair which gives rise to the greatest controversy.

There is a wide diversity of opinion among ethnologists on this question. Agassiz was followed by French writers, among whom were Topinard and Hervé, who held firmly to the plurality of centres of origin and distribution. Agassiz thought there were at least nine centres in which man appeared, each independent of the others. Morton thought he could point out twenty-two such centres, and Nott and Gliddon advanced the idea that there were distinct races of people. But Darwin, basing his arguments upon the uniformity of physical structure and similarity of mental characteristics, held that man came from a single progenitor. This theory is the most acceptable, and it is easily explained, if we admit time enough for the necessary changes in the structure and appearance of man. It is the simplest hypothesis that is given, and explains the facts relative to the existence of man much more easily than does the theory in reference to diversity of origins. The majority of ethnologists of America and Europe appear to favor the idea that man came from a single pair, arose from one place, and spread thence over the earth's surface.

The Primitive Home of Man May Be Determined in a General Way.—The location of the cradle of the race has not yet been satisfactorily established. The inference drawn from the Bible story of the creation places it in or near the valley of the Euphrates River. Others hold that the place was in Europe, and others still in America. A theory has also been advanced that a continent or group of large islands called Lemuria, occupying the place where the Indian Ocean now lies, and extending from Ceylon to Madagascar, was the locality in which the human race originated. The advocates of this theory hold to it chiefly on the ground that it is necessary to account for the peopling of Australia and other large islands and continents, and that it is the country best fitted by climate and other physical conditions for the primitive race. This submerged continent would enable the races to migrate readily to different parts of the world, still going by dry land.

There is little more than conjecture upon this subject, and the continent called Lemuria is as mythical as the Ethiopia of Ptolemy and the Atlantis of Plato. It is a convenient theory, as it places the cradle of the race near the five great rivers, the Tigris, Euphrates, Indus, Ganges, and the Nile. The supposed home also lies in a zone in which the animals most resembling man are found, which is an important consideration; as, in the development of the earth, animals appeared according to the conditions of climate and food supply, so the portion of the earth best prepared for man's early life is most likely to be his first home.

Although it is impossible to determine the first home of man, either from a scientific or an historical standpoint, there are a few well-acknowledged theories to be observed: First, as the islands of the ocean were not peopled when first discovered by modern navigators, it is reasonable to suppose that the primitive home of man was on one of the continents. As man is the highest and last development of organic nature, it is advocated, with considerable force of argument, that his first home was in a region suitable to the life of the anthropoid apes. As none of these, either living or fossil, are found in Australia or America, these continents are practically excluded from the probable list of places for the early home of man.

In considering the great changes which have taken place in the earth's surface, southern India and southern Africa were large islands at the time of man's appearance; hence, there is little probability of either of these being the primitive home. None of the oldest remains of man have been found in the high northern latitudes of Europe or America. We have then left a strip of country on the southern slope of the great mountain chain which begins in western Europe and extends to the Himalaya Mountains, in Asia, which appears to be the territory in which was situated the early home of man. The geological relics and the distribution of the race both point to the fact that in this belt man's life began; but it is not determined whether it was in Europe or in Asia, there being adherents to both theories.

The Antiquity of Man Is Shown in Racial Differentiation.—Granted that the life of the human race has originated from a common biological origin and from a common geographical centre, it has taken a very long time for the races to be differentiated into the physical traits they possess to-day, as it has taken a long time for man to spread over the earth. The generalized man wandering along the streams and through the forests in search of food, seeking for shelter under rocks and in caves and trees, was turned aside by the impassable barriers of mountains, or the forbidding glacier, the roaring torrent, or the limits of the ocean itself, and spread over the accessible parts of the earth's surface until he had covered the selected districts on the main portions of the globe. Then came race specialization, where a group remained a long time in the same environment and inbred in the same stock, developing specialized racial characters. These changes were very slow, and the wide difference to-day between the Asiatic, the African, and the European is indicative of the long period of years which brought them about. Certainly, six thousand years would not suffice to make such changes.

Of course one must realize that just as, in the period of childhood, the plastic state of life, changes of structure and appearance are more rapid than in the mature man, after traits and characters have become more fixed, so by analogy we may assume that this was the way of the human race and that in the earlier period changes were more rapid than they are to-day. Thus in the cross-fertilizations and amalgamation of races we would expect a slower development than under these earlier conditions, yet when we realize the persistence of the types of Irish and German, of Italian and Greek, of Japanese and Chinese, even though the races become amalgamated, we must infer that the racial types were very slow in developing.

If we consider the variations in the structure and appearance of the several tribes and races with which we come in contact in every-day life, we are impressed with the amount of time necessary to make these changes. Thus the Anglo-American, whom we sometimes call Caucasian, taken as one type of the perfection of physical structure and mental habit, with his brown hair, having a slight tendency to curl, his fair skin, high, prominent, and broad forehead, his great brain capacity, his long head and delicately moulded features, contrasts very strongly with the negro, with his black skin, long head, with flat, narrow forehead, thick lips, projecting jaw, broad nose, and black and woolly hair. The Chinese, with his yellow skin, flat nose, black, coarse hair, and oblique, almond-shaped eyes, and round skull, marks another distinct racial type. Other great races have different characteristics, and among our own race we find a further separation into two great types, the blonds and the brunettes.

What a long period of time must have elapsed to have changed the racial characteristics! From pictures made three thousand years ago in Egypt the differences of racial characteristics were very clearly depicted in the hair, the features of the face, and, indeed, the color of the skin. If at this period the racial differences were clearly marked, at what an early date must they have been wanting! So, also, the antiquity of man is evinced in the fact that the oldest skeletons found show him at that early period to be in possession of an average brain capacity and a well-developed frame. If changes in structure have taken place, they have gradually appeared only during a long period of years. Yet, when it is considered that man is a migratory creature, who can adapt himself to any condition of climate or other environment, and it is realized that in the early stage of his existence his time was occupied for a long period in hunting and fishing, and that from this practice he entered the pastoral life to continue, to a certain extent, his wanderings, it is evident that there is sufficient opportunity for the development of independent characteristics. Also the effects of sun and storm, of climate and other environments have a great influence in the slow changes of the race which have taken place. The change in racial traits is dependent largely upon biological selection, but environment and social selection probably had at least indirect influence in the evolution of racial characters.

The Evidences of Man's Ancient Life in Different Localities.—The sources of the remains of the life of primitive man are (1) Caves, (2) Shell Mounds, (3) River and Glacial Drift, (4) Burial Mounds, (5) Battlefields and Village Sites, and (6) Lake Dwellings. It is from these sources that most of the evidence of man's early life has come.

Caves (1).—It has been customary to allude to the cave man as if he were a distinct species or group of the human race, when in reality men at all times through many thousands of years dwelt in caves according to their convenience. However, there was a period in European life when groups of the human race used caves for permanent habitations and thus developed certain racial types and habits. Doubtless these were established long enough in permanent seats to develop a specialized type which might be known as the cave man, just as racial types have been developed in other conditions of habitation and life. What concerns us most here is that the protection which the cave afforded this primitive man has been a means of protecting the records of his life, and thus added to the evidence of human progress. Many of these caves were of limestone with rough walls and floor, and in most instances rifts in the roof allowed water to percolate and drop to the floor.

Frequently the water was impregnated with limestone solution, which became solidified as each drop left a deposit at the point of departure. This formed rough stalactites, which might be called stone icicles, because their formation was similar to the formation of an icicle of the water dropping from the roof. So likewise on the floor of the cave where the limestone solution dropped was built up from the bottom a covering of limestone with inverted stone icicles called stalagmites. Underneath the latter were found layer after layer of relics from the habitation of man, encased in stone to be preserved forever or until broken into by some outside pressure. Of course, comparatively few of all the relics around these habitations were preserved, because those outside of the stone encasement perished, as did undoubtedly large masses of remains around the mouth of the cave.

In these caves of Europe are found the bones of man, flint implements, ornaments of bone with carvings, and the necklaces of animals' teeth, along with the bones of extinct animals. In general the evidence shows the habits of the life of man and also the kind of animals with which he associated whose period of life was determined by other evidence. Besides this general evidence, there was a special determination of the progress of man, because the relics were in layers extending over a long period of years, giving evidence that from time to time implements of higher order were used, either showing progress or that different races may have occupied the cave at different times and left evidences of their industrial, economic, and social life. In some of the caves skulls have been discovered showing a brain case of an average capacity, along with others of inferior size. Probably the greater part of this cave life was in the upper part of the Paleolithic Stone Age.

In some of these caves at the time of the Magdalenian culture, which was a branch of the Crô-Magnon culture, there are to be found drawings and paintings of the horse, the cave bear, the mammoth, the bison, and many other animals, showing strong beginnings of representative art. Also, in these caves were found bones and stone implements of a more highly finished product than those of the earlier primitive types of Europe.

Shell Mounds (2).—Shell mounds of Europe and America furnish definite records of man's life. The shell mounds of greatest historic importance are found along the shores of the Baltic in Denmark. Here are remains of a primitive people whose diet seems to be principally shell-fish obtained from the shores of the sea. Around their kitchens the shells of mussels, scallops, and oysters were piled in heaps, and in these shell mounds, or Kitchenmiddens, as they are called (Kjokkenmoddings), are found implements, the bones of birds and mammals, as well as the remains of plants. Also, by digging to the bottom of these mounds specimens of pottery are found, showing that the civilization belonged largely to the Neolithic period of man.

There are evidences also of the succession of the varieties of trees corresponding to the evidences found in the peat bogs, the oak following the fir, which in turn gave way to the beech. These refuse heaps are usually in ridgelike mounds, sometimes hundreds of yards in length. The weight of the millions of shells and other refuse undoubtedly pressed the shells down into the soft earth and still the mound enlarged, the habitation being changed or raised higher, rather than to take the trouble to clear away the shells from the habitation. The variety of implements and the degrees of culture which they exhibit give evidence that men lived a long time in this particular locality. Undoubtedly it was the food quest that caused people to assemble here. The evidences of the coarse, dark pottery, the stone axes, clubs, and arrow-heads, and the bones of dogs show a state of civilization in which differentiation of life existed. Shell mounds are also found along the Pacific coast, showing the life of Indians from the time when they first began to use shell-fish for food. In these mounds implements showing the relative stages of development have been found.

River and Glacial Drift (3).—The action of glaciers and glacial rivers and lakes has through erosion changed the surface of the soil, tearing out some parts of the earth's surface and depositing the soil elsewhere. These river floods carried out bones of man and the implements in use, and deposited them, together with the bones of animals with which he lived. Many of these relics have been preserved through thousands of years and frequently are brought to light. The geological records are thus very important in throwing light upon the antiquity of man. It is in the different layers or strata of the earth caused by these changes that we find the relics of ancient life. The earth thus reveals in its rocks and gravel drift the permanent records of man's early life. Historical geology shows us that the crust of the earth has been made by a series of layers, one above the other, and that the geologist determining the order of their creation has a means of ascertaining their relative age, and thus can measure approximately the life of the plants and animals connected with each separate layer.[7] The relative ages of fishes, reptiles, and mammals, including man, are thus readily determined.

It is necessary to refer to the method of classification adopted by geologists, who have divided the time of earth-making into three great periods, representing the growth of animal life, determined by the remains found in the strata or drift. These periods mark general portions of time. Below the first is the period of earliest rock formation (Archaean), in which there is no life, and which is called Azoic for that reason. There is a short period above this, usually reckoned as outside the ancient life, on account of the few forms of animals found there; but the first great period (Paleozoic) represents non-vertebrate life, as well as the life of fishes and reptiles, and includes also the coal measures, which represent a period of heavy vegetation. The middle period (Mesozoic) includes the more completely developed lizards and crocodiles, and the appearance of mammals and birds. The animal life of the third period (Cenozoic) resembles somewhat the modern species. This period includes the Tertiary and the Quaternary and the recent sub-periods. Man, the highest being in the order of creation, appears in the Quaternary period. Of the immense ages of time represented by the geological periods the life of man represents but a small portion, just as the existence of man as recorded in history is but a modern period of his great life. The changes, then, which have taken place in the animals and plants and the climate in the different geological periods have been instrumental in determining the age of man; that is, if in a given stratum human remains are found, and the relative age of that stratum is known, it is easy to estimate the relative age of man.

Whether man existed prior to the glacial epoch is still in doubt. Some anthropologists hold that he appeared at the latter part of the Tertiary, that is, in the Pliocene. Reasons for assumption exist, though there is not sufficient evidence to make it conclusive. The question is still in controversy, and doubtless will be until new discoveries bring new evidence. If there is doubt about the finding of human relics in the Tertiary, there is no doubt about the evidence of man during the Quaternary, including the whole period of the glacial epoch, extending 500,000 years into the past.

The relics of man which are found in the drift and elsewhere are the stone implements and the flakes chipped from the flint as he fashioned it into an axe, knife, or hatchet. The implements commonly found are arrow-heads, knives, lance-heads, pestles, etc. Human bones have been found imbedded in the rock or the sand. Articles made of horn, bones of animals, especially the reindeer, notched or cut pieces of wood have been found. Also there are evidences of rude drawings on stone, bone, or ivory; fragments of charcoal, which give evidence of the use of fire in cooking or creating artificial heat, are found, and long bones split longitudinally to obtain marrow for food, and, finally, the remnants of pottery. These represent the principal relics found in the Stone Age; to these may be added the implements in bronze and iron of later periods.

A good example of the use of these relics to determine chronology is shown in the peat bogs of Denmark. At the bottom are found trees of pine which grew on the edges of the bog and have fallen in. Nearer the top are found oak and white birch-trees, and in the upper layer are found beech-trees closely allied to the species now covering the country. The pines, oaks, and birches are not to be seen in that part of the country at present. Here, then, is evidence of the successive replacement of different species of trees. It is evident that it must have taken a long time for one species thus to replace another, but how long it is impossible to say. In some of these bogs is found a gradation of implements, unpolished stone at the bottom, polished stone above, followed by bronze, and finally iron. These are associated with the different forms of vegetable remains.

In Europe stone implements occur in association with fossil remains of the cave lion, the cave hyena, the old elephant and rhinoceros—all extinct species. Also the bones and horns of the reindeer are prominent in these remains, for at that time the reindeer came farther south than at present. In southern France similar implements are associated with ivory and bones, with rude markings, and the bones of man—even a complete skeleton being found at one place. These are all found in connection with the bones of the elk, ibex, aurochs, and reindeer.

Burial Mounds (4).—It is difficult to determine at just what period human beings began to bury their dead. Primarily the bodies were disposed of the same as any other carrion that might occur—namely, they were left to decay wherever they dropped, or were subject to the disposal by wild animals. After the development of the idea of the perpetuation of life in another world, even though it were temporary or permanent, thoughts of preparing the body for its journey into the unknown land and for its residence thereafter caused people to place food and implements and clothing in the grave. This practice probably occurred about the beginning of the Neolithic period of man's existence, and has continued on to the present date.

Hence it is that in the graves of primitive man we find deposited the articles of daily use at the period in which he lived. These have been preserved many centuries, showing something of the life of the people whose remains were deposited in the mounds. Also in connection with this in furtherance of a religious idea were great dolmens and stone temples, where undoubtedly the ancients met to worship. They give some evidence at least of the development of the religious and ceremonial life among these primitive people and to that extent they are of great importance. It is evidence also, in another way, that the religious idea took strong hold of man at an early period of his existence. Evidences of man in Britain from the tumuli, or burial mounds, from rude stone temples like the famous Stonehenge place his existence on the island at a very early date. Judging from skulls and skeletons there were several distinct groups of prehistoric man in Britain, varying from the extreme broad skulls to those of excessive length. They carry us back to the period of the Early Stone Age. Relics, too, of the implements and mounds show something of the primitive conditions of the inhabitants in Britain of which we have any permanent record.

Battlefields and Village Sites (5).—In the later Neolithic period of man the tribes had been fully developed over a great part of the earth's surface, and fought for their existence, principally over territories having a food supply. Other reasons for tribal conflict, such as real or imagined race differences and the ambition for race survival, caused constant warfare. Upon these battlefields were left the implements of war. Those of stone, and, it may be said secondarily, of iron and bronze, were preserved. It is not uncommon now in almost any part of the United States where the rains fall upon a ploughed field over which a battle had been fought, to find exposed a large number of arrow-heads and stone axes, all other perishable implements having long since decayed. Or in some instances the wind blowing the sand exposes the implements which were long ago deposited during a battle. Also, wherever the Indian villages were located for a period of years, the accumulations of utensils and implements occurred which were buried by the action of wind or water. This represents a source of evidence of man's early life.

Lake Dwellings (6).—The idea of protection is evidenced everywhere in the history of primitive man; protection against the physical elements, protection against wild beasts and wilder men. We find along the lakes and bays in both Europe and America the tendency to build the dwelling out in the water and approach it from the land with a narrow walk which could be taken up when not used, or to approach it by means of a rude boat. In this way the dwellers could defend themselves against the onslaughts of tribal enemies. These dwellings have been most numerous along the Swiss lakes, although some are found in Scotland, in the northern coast of South America, and elsewhere. Their importance rests in the fact that, like the shell mounds (Kitchenmiddens), the refuse from these cabins shows large deposits of the implements and utensils that were in use during the period of tribal residence. Here we find not only stone implements, running from the crude form of the Unpolished Stone Age to the highly polished, but also records of implements of bronze and small implements for domestic use of bone and polished stone. Also there are evidences that different tribes or specialized races occupied these dwellings at different times, because of the variation of civilization implied by the implements in use. The British Museum has a very large classified collection of the implements procured from lake dwellings of Switzerland. Other museums also have large collections. A part of them run back into the prehistoric period of man and part extend even down to the historic.

Knowledge of Man's Antiquity Influences Reflective Thinking.—The importance of studying the antiquity of man is the light which it throws upon the causes of later civilization. In considering any phase of man's development it is necessary to realize he has been a long time on earth and that, while the law of the individual life is development, that of the human race is slowly evolutionary; hence, while we may look for immediate and rapid change, we can only be assured of a very slow progressive movement at all periods of man's existence. The knowledge of his antiquity will give us a historical view which is of tremendous importance in considering the purpose and probable result of man's life on earth. When we realize that we have evidence of the struggle of man for five hundred thousand years to get started as far as we have in civilization, and that more changes affecting man's progress may occur in a single year now than in a former thousand years, we realize something of the background of struggle before our present civilization could appear. We realize, also, that his progress in the arts has been very slow and that, while there are many changes in art formation of to-day, we still have the evidences of the primitive in every completed picture, or plastic form, or structural work. But the slow progress of all this shows, too, that the landmarks of civilization of the past are few and far between—distant mile-posts appearing at intervals of thousands of years. Such a contemplation gives us food for thought and should invite patience when we wish in modern times for social transformations to become instantaneous, like the flash of the scimitar or the burst of an electric light.

The evidence that man has been a long time on earth explodes the long-accepted theory of six thousand years as the age of man. It also explodes the theory of instantaneous creation which was expressed by some of the mediaeval philosophers. Indeed, it explodes the theory of a special creation of man without connection with the creation of other living beings. No doubt, there was a specialized creation of man, otherwise he never would have been greater than the anthropoids nor, indeed, than other mammals, but his specialization came about as an evolutionary process which gave him a tremendous brain-power whereby he was enabled to dominate all the rest of the world. So far as philosophy is concerned as to man's life, purpose, and destiny, the influence of the study of anthropology would change the philosopher's vision of life to a certain extent. The recognition that man is "part and parcel" of the universe, subject to cosmic law, as well as a specialized type, subject to the laws of evolution, and, indeed, that he is of a spiritual nature through which he is subjected to spiritual law, causes the philosopher to pause somewhat before he determines the purpose, the life, or the destiny of man.

If we are to inquire how man came into the world, when he came, what he has been doing, how he developed, and whither the human trail leads, we shall encounter many unsolved theories. Indeed, the facts of his life are suggestive of the mystery of being. If it be suggested that he is "part and parcel" of nature and has slowly arisen out of lower forms, it should not be a humiliating thought, for his daily life is dependent upon the lower elements of nature. The life of every day is dependent upon the dust of the earth. The food he eats comes from the earth just the same as that of the hog, the rabbit, or the fish. If, upon this foundation, he has by slow evolution built a more perfect form, developed a brain and a mind which give him the greatest flights of philosophy, art, and religion, is it not a thing to excite pride of being? Could there be any greater miracle than evolving nature and developing life? Indeed, is there any greater than the development of the individual man from a small germ not visible to the naked eye, through the egg, the embryo, infant, youth, to full-grown man? Why not the working of the same law to the development of man from the beginning. Does it lessen the dignity of creation if this is done according to law? On the other hand, does it not give credit to the greatness and power of the Creator if we recognize his wisdom in making the universe, including man, the most important factor, according to a universal plan worked out by far-reaching laws?

SUBJECTS FOR FURTHER STUDY

1. Evidences of the great antiquity of man.

2. Physical and mental traits of the anthropoid apes.

3. The life and culture of the Neanderthal Race.

4. What are the evidences in favor of the descent of man from a single progenitor?

5. Explain the law of differentiation as applied to plants and animals.

6. Compare in general the arts of man in the Old Stone Age with those of the New Stone Age.

7. What has been the effect of the study of prehistoric man on modern thought as shown in the interpretation of History? Philosophy? Religion?

[1] See Diagram, p. 59.

[2] See Haeckel, Schmidt, Ward, Robinson, Osborn, Todd.

[3] See Osborn, *Men of the Old Stone Age*.

[4] See Chapter II.

[5] After Osborn. Read from bottom up.

[6] Estimates of Neanderthal vary from 150,000 to 50,000 years ago.

[7] See p. 64.

CHAPTER V

THE ECONOMIC FACTORS OF PROGRESS

The Efforts of Man to Satisfy Physical Needs.—All knowledge of primitive man, whether derived from the records of cultures he has left or assumed from analogy of living tribes of a low order of civilization, discovers him wandering along the streams in the valleys or by the shores of lakes and oceans, searching for food and incidentally seeking protection in caves and trees. The whole earth was his so far as he could appropriate it. He cared nothing for ownership; he only wanted room to search for the food nature had provided. When he failed to find sufficient food as nature left it, he starved. So in his wandering life he adapted himself to nature as he found it. In the different environments he acquired different customs and habits of life. If he came in contact with other tribes, an exchange of knowledge and customs took place, and both tribes were richer thereby. However, the universality of the human mind made it possible for two detached tribes, under similar environment and similar stimuli, to develop the same customs and habits of life, provided they had the same degree of development. Hence, we have independent group development and group borrowing.

When nature failed to provide him with sufficient food, he learned to force her to yield a larger supply. When natural objects were insufficient for his purposes, he made artificial tools to supplement them. Slowly he became an inventor. Slowly he mastered the art of living. Thus physical needs were gradually satisfied, and the foundation for the superstructure of civilization was laid.

The Attempt to Satisfy Hunger and to Protect from Cold.—To this statement must be added the fact that struggle with his fellows arose from the attempt to obtain food, and we have practically the whole occupation of man in a state of savagery. At least, the simple activities represent the essential forces at the foundation of human social life. The attempt to preserve life either through instinct, impulse, emotion, or rational selection is fundamental in all animal existence. The other great factor at the foundation of human effort is the desire to perpetuate the species. This, in fact, is the mere projection of the individual life into the next generation, and is fundamentally important to the individual and to the race alike. All modern efforts can be traced to these three fundamental activities. But in seeking to satisfy the cravings of hunger and to avoid the pain of cold, man has developed a varied and active life. About these two centres cluster all the simple forces of human progress. Indeed, invention and discovery and the advancement of the industrial arts receive their initial impulses from these economic relations.

We have only to turn our attention to the social life around us to observe evidences of the great importance of economic factors. Even now it will be observed that the greater part of economic activities proceeds from the effort to procure food, clothing, and shelter, while a relatively smaller part is engaged in the pursuit of education, culture, and pleasure. The excellence of educational systems, the highest flights of philosophy, the greatest achievement of art, and the best inspiration of religion cannot exist without a wholesome economic life at the foundation. It should not be humiliating to man that this is so, for in the constitution of things, labor of body and mind, the struggle for existence and the accumulations of the products of industry yield a large return in themselves in discipline and culture; and while we use these economic means to reach higher ideal states, they represent the ladder on which man makes the first rounds of his ascent.

The Methods of Procuring Food in Primitive Times.—Judging from the races and tribes that are more nearly in a state of nature than any other, it may be reasonably assumed that in his first stage of existence, man subsisted almost wholly upon a vegetable diet, and that gradually he gave more and more attention to animal food. His structure and physiology make it possible for him to use both animal and vegetable food. Primarily, with equal satisfaction the procuring of food must have been rather an individual than a social function. Each individual sought his own breakfast wherever he might find it. It was true then, as now, that people proceeded to the breakfast table in an aggregation, and flocked around the centres of food supply; so we may assume the picture of man stealing away alone, picking fruits, nuts, berries, gathering clams or fish, was no more common than the fact of present-day man getting his own breakfast alone. The main difference is that in the former condition individuals obtained the food as nature left it, and passed it directly from the bush or tree to the mouth, while in modern times thousands of people have been working indirectly to make it possible for a man to wait on himself.

Jack London, in his *Before Adam*, gives a very interesting picture of the tribe going out to the carrot field for its breakfast, each individual helping himself. However, such an aggregation around a common food supply must eventually lead to co-operative economic methods. But we do find even among modern living tribes of low degree of culture the group following the food quest, whether it be to the carrot patch, the nut-bearing trees, the sedgy seashore for mussels and clams, the lakes for wild rice, or to the forest and plains where abound wild game.

We find it difficult to think otherwise than that the place of man's first appearance was one abounding in edible fruits. This fact arises from the study of man's nature and evidences of the location of his first appearance, together with the study of climate and vegetation. There are a good many suggestions also that man in his primitive condition was prepared for a vegetable diet, and indications are that later he acquired use of meat as food. Indeed, the berries and edible roots of certain regions are in sufficient quantity to sustain life throughout a greater part of the year. The weaker tribes of California at the time of the first European invaders, and for many centuries previous, found a greater part of their sustenance in edible roots extracted from the soil, in nuts, seeds of wild grains, and grasses. It is true they captured a little wild game, and in certain seasons many of them made excursions to the ocean or frequented the streams for fish or shell-fish, but their chief diet was vegetable. It must be remembered, also, that all of the cultivated fruits to-day formerly existed, in one variety or another, in the wild species. Thus the citrous fruits, the date, the banana, breadfruit, papaw, persimmon, apple, cherry, plum, pear, all grew in a wild state, providing food for man if he were ready to take it as provided. Rational selection has assisted nature in improving the quality of grains and fruits and in developing new varieties.

In the tropical regions was found the greatest supply of edible fruits. Thus the Malays and the Papuans find sufficient food on trees to supply their wants. Many people in some of the groups in the South Sea Islands live on cocoanuts. In South America several species of trees are cultivated by the natives for the food they furnish. The palm family contributes much food to the natives, and also furnishes a large supply of food to the markets of the world. The well-known breadfruit tree bears during eight successive months in the year, and by burying the fruit in the ground it may be preserved for food for the remaining four months. Thus a single plant may be made to provide a continuous food supply for the inhabitants of the Moluccas and Philippines. Many other instances of fruits in abundance, such as the nuts from the araucarias of South America, and beans from the mesquite of Mexico, might be given to show that it is possible for man to subsist without the use of animal food.

The Variety of Food Was Constantly Increased.—Undoubtedly, one of the chief causes of the wandering of primitive man over the earth, in the valleys, along stream, lake, and ocean, over the plains and through the hills, was the quest for food to preserve life; and even after tribes became permanent residents in a certain territory, there was a constant shifting from one source of food supply to another throughout the seasons. However, after tribes became more settled, the increase of population encroached upon the native food supply, and man began to use his invention for the purpose of its increase. He learned how to plant seeds which were ordinarily believed to be sown by the gods, and to till the soil and raise fruits and vegetables for his own consumption. This was a period of accidental agriculture, or hoe culture, whereby the ground was tilled by women with hoes of stone, or bone, or wood. In the meantime, the increase of animal food became a necessity. Man learned how to snare and trap animals, to fish and to gather shell-fish, learning by degrees to use new foods as discovered as nature left them. Life become a veritable struggle for existence as the population increased and the lands upon which man dwelt yielded insufficient supply of food. The increased variety of food allowed man to adapt himself to the different climates. Thus in the colder climates animal food became desirable to enable him to resist more readily the rigors of climate. It was not necessary, it is supposed, to give him physical courage or intellectual development, for there appear to be evidences of tribes like the Maoris of New Zealand, who on the diet of fish and roots became a most powerful and sagacious people. But the change from a vegetable diet to a meat-and-fish diet in the early period brought forth renewed energy of body and mind, not only on account of the necessary physical exertion but on account of the invention of devices for the capture of fish and game.

The Food Supply Was Increased by Inventions.—Probably the first meat food supply was in the form of shell-fish which could be gathered near the shores of lakes and streams. Probably small game was secured by the use of stones and sticks and by running the animal down until he was exhausted or until he hid in a place inaccessible to the pursuer. The boomerang, as used by the Australians in killing game, may have been an early product of the people of Neolithic Europe. In the latter part of the Paleolithic Age, fish-hooks of bone were used, and probably snares invented for small game. The large game could not be secured without the use of the spear and the co-operation of a number of hunters. In all probability this occurred in the New Stone Age.

The invention of the bow-and-arrow was of tremendous importance in securing food. It is not known what led to its invention, although the discovery of the flexible power of the shrub, or the small sapling, must have occurred to man as he struggled through the brush. It is thought by some that the use of the bow fire-drill, which was for the purpose of striking fire by friction, might have displayed driving power when the drill wound up in the string of the bow flew from its confinement. However, this is conjectural; but, judging from the inventions of known tribes, it is evident that necessity has always been the moving power in invention. The bow-and-arrow was developed in certain centres and probably through trade and exchange extended to other tribes and groups until it was universally used.

It is interesting to note how many thousands of years this must have been the chief weapon for destroying animals or crippling game at a distance. Even as late as the Norman conquest, the bow-and-arrow was the chief means of defense of the Anglo-Saxon yeoman, and for many previous centuries in the historic period had been the chief implement in warfare and in the chase. The use of the spear in fishing supplemented that of the hook, and is found among all low-cultured tribes of the present day. The American Indian will stand on a rock in the middle of a stream, silently, for an hour if necessary, watching for a chance to spear a salmon. These small devices were of tremendous importance in increasing the food supply, and the making of them became a permanent industry.

Along with the bow and arrow were developed many kinds of spears, axes, and hammers, invented chiefly to be used in war, but also used for economic reasons. In the preparation of animal food, in the tanning of skins, in the making of clothing, another set of stone implements was developed. So, likewise, in the grinding of seeds, the mortar and pestle were used, and the small hand-mill or grinder was devised. The sign of the mortar and pestle at the front of drug-stores brings to mind the fact that its first use was not for preparing medicines, but for grinding grains and seeds.

The Discovery and Use of Fire.—The use of fire was practised in the early history of man. Among the earliest records in caves are found evidences of the use of fire. Charcoal is practically indestructible, and, although it may be crushed, the small particles maintain their shape in the clays and sands. In nearly all of the relics of man discovered in caves, the evidences of fire are to be found, and no living tribe has yet been discovered so low in the scale of life as to be without the knowledge of fire and probably its simple uses, although a few tribes have been for the time being without fire when first discovered. This might seem to indicate that at a very early period man did not know how to create fire artificially, but carried it and preserved it in his wanderings. There are indications that a certain individual was custodian of the fire, and later it was carried by the priest or *cacique*. Here, as in other instances in the development of the human race, an economic factor soon assumes a religious significance, and fire becomes sacred.

There are many conjectures respecting the discovery of fire. Probably the two real sources are of lightning that struck forest trees and set them on fire and the action of volcanoes in throwing out burning lava, which ignited combustible material. Either one or the other, and perhaps both, of these methods may have furnished man with fire. Others have suggested that the rubbing together of dead limbs of trees in the forests after they were moved by the winds, may have created fire by friction. It is possible, also, that the sun's rays may have, when concentrated on combustible material, caused spontaneous ignition. The idea has been advanced that some of the forest fires of recent times have been ignited in this way. However, it is evident that there are enough natural sources in the creation of fire to enable tribes to use it for the purposes of artificial heat, cooking, and later, in the age of metals, of smelting ores.

There has always been a mystery connected with the origin and use of fire, which has led to many myths. Thus, the Greeks insisted that Prometheus, in order to perform a great service to humanity, stole fire from heaven and gave it to man. For this crime against the authority of the gods, he was chained to a rock to suffer the torture of the vulture who pecked at his vitals. Aeschylus has made the most of this old legend in his great drama of *Prometheus Bound.* Nearly every tribe or nation has some tradition regarding the origin of fire. Because of its mystery and its economic value, it was early connected with religion and made sacred in many instances. It was thus preserved at the altar, never being allowed to become extinct without the fear of dire calamity. Perhaps the economic and religious ideas combined, because tribes in travelling from place to place exercised great care to preserve it. The use of fire in worship became almost universal among tribes and ancient nations. Thus the Hebrews and the Aryans, including Greeks, Romans, and Persians, as well as the Chinese and Japanese, used fire in worship. Among other tribes it was worshipped as a symbol or even as a real deity. Even in the Christian religion, the use of the burning incense may have some psychological connection with the idea of purification through fire. Whether its mysterious nature led to its connection with worship, and the superstition connected with its continued burning, or whether from economic reasons it became a sacred matter, has never been determined. The custom that a fire should never go out upon the altar, and that it should be carried in migrations from place to place, would seem to indicate that these two motives were closely allied, if not related in cause and effect.

Evidently, fire was used for centuries before man invented methods of reproducing it. Simple as the process involved, it was a great invention; or it may be stated that many devices were resorted to for the creation of artificial fire. Perhaps the earliest was that of rubbing two pieces of dry wood together, producing fire by friction. This could be accomplished by persistent friction of two ordinary pieces of dry wood, or by drilling a hole in a dry piece of wood with a pointed stick until heat was developed and a spark produced to ignite pieces of dry bark or grass. Another way was to make a groove in a block of wood and run the end of a stick rapidly back and forth through the groove. An invention called the fire-drill was simply a method of twirling rapidly in the hand a wooden drill which was in contact with dry wood, or by winding a string of the bow several times around the drill and moving the bow back and forth horizontally, giving rapid motion to the drill.

As tribes became more advanced, they used two pieces of flint with which to strike fire, and after the discovery of iron, the flint and iron were used. How many centuries these simple devices were essential to the progress and even to the life of tribes, is not known; but when we realize that but a few short years ago our fathers lighted the fire with flint and steel, and that before the percussion cap was invented, the powder in the musket was ignited by flint and hammer, we see how important to civilization were these simple devices of producing fire artificially. So simple an invention as the discovery of the friction match saved hours of labor and permitted hours of leisure to be used in other ways. It is one of the vagaries of human progress that a simple device remains in use for thousands of years before its clumsy method gives way to a new invention only one step in advance of the old.

Cooking Added to the Economy of the Food Supply.—Primitive man doubtless consumed his food raw. The transition of the custom of uncooked food to cooked food must have been gradual. We only know that many of the backward tribes of to-day are using primitive methods of cooking, and the man of the Stone Ages had methods of cooking the meat of animals. In all probability, the suggestion came as people were grouped around the fire for artificial heat, and then, either by intention or desire, the experiment of cooking began. After man had learned to make water-tight baskets, a common device of cooking was to put water in the basket and, after heating stones on a fire, put them in the basket to heat the water and then place the food in the basket to be cooked. This method is carried on by the Indians in some parts of Alaska to this day, where they use a water-tight basket for this purpose. Probably this method of cooking food was a later development than the roasting of food on coals or in the ashes, or in the use of the wooden spit. Catlin, in his *North American Indians*, relates that certain tribes of Indians dig a hole in the ground and line it with hide filled with water, then place hot stones in the water, in which they place their fish, game, or meat for cooking. This is interesting, because it carries out a more or less universal idea of adaptation to environment. Probably the plains Indians had no baskets or other vessels to use for this purpose, but they are found to have used similar methods of cooking grasshoppers. They dig a hole in the ground, build a fire in the hole, and take the fire out and put in the grasshoppers. Thus, they have an exhibition of the first fireless cooker.

It is thought by some that the need of vessels which would endure the heat was the cause of the invention of pottery. While there seems to be little evidence of this, it is easy to conjecture that when water was needed to be heated in a basket, a mass of clay would be put on the bottom of the basket before it was put over the coals of fire. After the cooking was done, the basket could easily be detached from the clay, leaving a hard-baked bowl. This led to the suggestion of making bowls of clay and baking them for common use. Others suggest that the fact of making holes in the ground for cooking purposes gave the suggestion that by the use of clay a portable vessel might be made for similar purposes.

The economic value of cooking rests in the fact that a larger utility comes from the cooked than from the raw food. Though the phenomena of physical development of tribes and nations cannot be explained by the chemical constituents of food, although they are not without a positive influence. Evidently the preparation of food has much to do with man's progress, and the art of cooking was a great step in advance. The better utilization of food was a time-saving process—and, indeed, in many instances may have been a life-saving affair.

The Domestication of Animals.—The time and place of the domestication of animals are not satisfactorily determined. We know that Paleolithic man had domesticated the dog, and probably for centuries this was the only animal domesticated; but it is known that low forest tribes have tamed monkeys and parrots for pets, and savage tribes frequently have a band of dogs for hunting game or guarding the hut. While it may be supposed that domestication of animals may have occurred in the prehistoric period, the use of such animals has been in the historic period. There are many evidences of the domesticated dog at the beginning of the

Neolithic period. However, these animals may have still been nearly half wild. It is not until the period of the Lake Dwellings of Switzerland that we can discriminate between the wild animals and those that have been tamed. In the Lake Dwelling débris are found the bones of the wild bull, or *urus*, of Europe. Probably this large, long-horned animal was then in a wild state, and had been hunted for food. Alongside of these remains are those of a small, short-horned animal, supposed to have been domesticated. Later, though still in the Neolithic period, remains of short-horned tame cattle appear in the refuse of the Lake Dwellings. It is thought by some that these two varieties—the long-horned *urus* and the short-horned domesticated animal brought from the south—were crossed, which gave rise to the origin of the present stock of modern cattle in central Europe. Pigs and sheep were probably domesticated in Asia and brought into Europe during the later Neolithic or early Bronze period.

The horse was domesticated in Asia, and Clark Wissler[1] shows that to be one great centre of cultural distribution for this animal. It spread from Asia into Europe, and from Europe into America. The llama was early domesticated in South America. The American turkey had its native home in Mexico, the hen in Asia. The dog, though domesticated very early in Asia, has gone wherever the human race has migrated, as the constant companion of man. The horse, while domesticated in Asia, depends upon the culture of Europe for his large and extended use, and has spread over the world. We find that in the historic period the Aryan people everywhere made use of the domesticated goat, horse, and dog. In the northern part of Europe, the reindeer early became of great service to the inhabitants for milk, meat, and clothing. The great supply of milk and meat from domesticated animals added tremendously to the food supply of the race, and made it possible for it to develop in other lines. Along with the food supply has been the use of these animals for increasing the clothing supply through hides, furs, skins, and wool. The domestication of animals laid the foundation for great economic advancement.

The Beginnings of Agriculture Were Very Meagre.—Man had gathered seeds and fruit and berries for many years before he conceived the notion of planting seeds and cultivating crops. It appears to be a long time before he knew enough to gather seeds and plant them for a harvest. Having discovered this, it was only necessary to have the will and energy to prepare the soil, sow the seed, and harvest a crop in order to enter upon agriculture. But to learn this simple act must have required many crude experiments. In the migrations of mankind they adopted a little intermittent agriculture, planting the grains while the tribe paused for pasture of flocks and herds, and resting long enough for a crop to be harvested. They gradually began to supplement the work of the pastoral with temporary agriculture, which was used as a means of supplementing the food supply. It was not until people settled in permanent habitations and ceased their pastoral wanderings that real agriculture became established. Even then it was a crude process, and, like every other economic industry of ancient times, its development was excessively slow.

The wandering tribes of North America at the time of the discovery had reached the state of raising an occasional crop of corn. Indeed, some tribes were quite constant in limited agriculture. The sedentary Indians of New Mexico, old Mexico, and Peru also cultivated corn and other plants, as did those of Central America. The first tillage of the soil was meagre, and the invention of agricultural implements proceeded slowly. At first wandering savages carried a pointed stick to dig up the roots and tubers used for food. The first agriculturists used sticks for stirring the soil, which finally became flattened in the form of a paddle or rude spade. The hoe was evolved from the stone pick or hatchet. It is said that the women of the North American tribes used a hoe made of an elk's shoulder-blade and a handle of wood. In Sweden the earliest records of tillage represent a huge hoe made from a stout limb of spruce with the sharpened root. This was finally made heavier, and men dragged it through the soil in the manner of ploughing. Subsequently the plough was made in two pieces, a handle having been added. Finally a pair of cows yoked together were compelled to drag the plough. Probably this is a fair illustration of the manner of the evolution of the plough in other countries. It is also typical of the evolution of all modern agricultural implements.

We need only refer to our own day to see how changes take place. The writer has cut grain with the old-fashioned sickle, the scythe, the cradle, and the reaper, and has lived to see the harvester cut and thresh the grain in the field. The Egyptians use until this day wooden ploughs of an ancient type formed from limbs of trees, having a share pointed with metal. The old Spanish colonists used a similar plough in California and Mexico as late as the nineteenth century. From these ploughs, which merely stirred the soil imperfectly, there has been a slow evolution to the complete steel plough and disk of modern times. A glance at the collection of perfected farm machinery at any modern agricultural fair reveals what man has accomplished since the beginning of the agricultural art. In forest countries the beginning of agriculture was in the open places, or else the natives cut and burned the brush and timber, and frequently, after one or two crops, moved on to other places. The early settlers of new territories pursue the same method with their first fields, while the turning of the prairie sod of the Western plains was frequently preceded by the burning of the prairie grass and brush.

The method of attachment to the soil determined economic progress. Man in his early wanderings had no notion of ownership of the land. All he wished was to have room to go wherever the food quest directed him, and apparently he had no reflections on the subject. The matters of fact regarding mountain, sea, river, ocean, and glacier which influenced his movements were practically no different from the fact of other tribes that barred his progress or interfered with his methods of life. In the hunter-fisher stage of existence, human contacts became frequent, and led to contention and warfare over customary hunting grounds. Even in the pastoral period the land was occupied by moving upon it, and held as long as the tribe could maintain itself against other tribes that wished the land for pasture. Gradually, however, even in temporary locations, a more permanent attachment to the soil came through clusters of dwellings and villages, and the habit of using territory from year to year for pastorage led to a claim of the tribe for that territory. So the idea of possession grew into the idea of permanent ownership and the idea of rights to certain parts of the territory became continually stronger. This method of settlement had much to do with not only the economic life of people, but in determining the nature of their social organizations and consequently the efficiency of their social activity. Evidently, the occupation of a certain territory as a dwelling-place was the source of the idea of ownership in land.

Nearly all of Europe, at least, came into permanent cultivation through the village community.[2] A tribe settled in a given valley and held the soil in common. There was at a central place an irregular collection of rude huts, called the village. Each head of the family owned and permanently occupied one of these. The fertile or tillable land was laid out in lots, each family being allowed the use of a lot for one or more years, but the whole land was the common property of the tribe, and was under the direction of the village elders. The regulation of the affairs of the agricultural community developed government, law, and social cohesion. The social advancement after the introduction of permanent agriculture was great in every way. The increased food supply was an untold blessing; the closer association necessary for the new kind of life, the building of distinct homes, and the necessity of a more general citizenship and a code of public law brought forth the social or community idea of progress. Side by side with the village community system there was a separate development of individual ownership and tillage, which developed into the manorial system. It is not necessary to discuss this method here except to say that this, together with the permanent occupation of the house-lot in the village, gave rise to the private ownership of property in land. As to how private ownership of personal property began, it is easy to suppose that, having made an implement or tool, the person claimed the right of perpetual possession or ownership; also, that in the chase the captured game belonged to the one who made the capture; the clothing to the maker. In some instances where game was captured by the group, each was given a share in proportion to his station in life, or again in proportion to the service each performed in the capture. Yet, in this early period possessory right was frequently determined on the basis that might makes right.

The Manufacture of Clothing.—The motive of clothing has been that of ornament and protection from the pain of cold. The ornamentation of the body was earlier in its appearance in human progress than the making of clothing for the protection of the body; and after the latter came into use, ornamentation continued, thus making clothing more and more artistic. As to how man protected his body before he began to kill wild animals for food, is conjectural. Probably he dwelt in a warm climate, where very little clothing was needed, but, undoubtedly, the cave man and, in fact, all of the groups of the race occurring in Europe and Asia in the latter part of the Old

Stone Age and during the New Stone Age used the skins of animals for clothing. Later, after weaving had begun, grasses and fibres taken from plants in a rude way were plaited for making clothing. Subsequently these fibres were prepared, twisted into thread, and woven regularly into garments. The main source of supply came from reeds, rushes, wild flax, cotton, fibres of the century plant, the inner bark of trees, and other sources according to the environment.

Nothing can be more interesting than the progress made in clothing, combining as it does the objects of protection from cold, the adornment of the person, and the preservation of modesty. Indians of the forests of the tropical regions and on the Pacific coast, when first discovered, have been found entirely naked. These were usually without modesty. That is, they felt no need of clothing on account of the presence of others. There are many evidences to show that the first clothing was for ornament and for personal attraction rather than for protection. The painting of the body, the dressing of the hair, the wearing of rings in the nose, ears, and lips, the tattooing of the body, all are to be associated with the first clothing, which may be merely a narrow belt or an ornamental piece of cloth—all merely for show, for adornment and attraction.

There are relics of ornaments found in caves of early man, and, as before mentioned, relics of paints. The clothing of early man can be conjectured by the implements with which he was accustomed to dress the skins of animals. Among living tribes the bark of trees represents the lowest form of clothing. In Brazil there is found what is known as the "shirt tree," which provides covering for the body. When a man wants a new garment he pulls the bark from a tree of a suitable size, making a complete girdle. This he soaks and beats until it is soft, and, cutting holes for the arms, dons his tailor-made garment. In some countries, particularly India, aprons are made of leaves. But the garment made of the skins of animals is the most universal among living savage and barbarous tribes, even after the latter have learned to spin and weave fabrics. The tanning of skins is carried on with a great deal of skill, and rich and expensive garments are worn by the wealthier members of savage tribes.

The making of garments from threads, strings, or fibres was an art discovered a little later. At first rude aprons were woven from long strips of bark. The South Sea Islanders made short gowns of plaited rushes, and the New Zealanders wore rude garments from strings made of native flax. These early products were made by the process of working the fibres by hand into a string or thread. The use of a simple spindle, composed of a stone like a large button, with a stick run through a hole in the centre, facilitated the making of thread and the construction of rude looms. It was but a step from these to the spinning-wheels and looms of the Middle Ages. When the Spaniards discovered the Pueblo Indians, they were wearing garments of their own weaving from cotton and wood fibres. Strong cords attached to the limbs of trees and to a piece of wood on the ground formed the framework of the loom, and the native sat down to weave the garment. With slight improvements on this old style, the Navajos continue to weave their celebrated blankets. What an effort it must have cost, what a necessity must have crowded man to have compelled him to resort to this method of procuring clothing!

The artistic taste in dress has always accompanied the development of the useful, although dress has always been used more or less for ornament, and taste has changed by slow degrees. The primitive races everywhere delighted in bright colors, and in most instances these border on the grotesque in arrangement and combination. But many people not far advanced in barbarism have colors artistically arranged and dress with considerable skill. Ornaments change in the progress of civilization from coarse, ungainly shells, pieces of wood, or bits of metal, to more finely wrought articles of gold and silver.

Primitive Shelters and Houses.—The shelters of primitive man were more or less temporary, for wherever he happened to be in his migrations he sought shelter from storm or cold in the way most adaptable to his circumstances. There was in this connection, also, the precaution taken to protect against predatory animals and wild men. As his stay in a given territory became more permanent, the home or shelter gradually grew more permanent. So far as we can ascertain, man has always been known to build some sort of shelter. As apes build their shelters in trees, birds build their nests, and beavers dam water to make their homes, it is impossible to suppose that man, with superior intelligence, was ever simple enough to continue long without some sort of shelter constructed with his own hands. At first the shelter of trees, rocks, and caves served his purpose wherever available. Subsequently, when he had learned to build houses, their structure was usually dependent more upon environment than upon his inventive genius. Whether he built a platform house or nest in a tree, or provided a temporary brush shelter, or bark hut, or stone or adobe building, depended a good deal upon the material at hand and the necessity of protection. The main thing was to protect against cold or storm, wild animals, and, eventually, wild men.

The progress in architecture among the nations of ancient civilization was quite rapid. Massive structures were built for capacity and strength, which the natives soon learned to decorate within and without. The buildings were made of large blocks of hewn stone, fitted together mechanically by the means of cement, which made secure foundations for ages. When in the course of time the arch was discovered, it alone became a power to advance the progress of architecture. We have seen pass before our eyes a sudden transition in dwelling houses.

The first inhabitants of some parts of the Western prairies dwelt in tents. These were next exchanged for the "dugout," and this for a rude hut. Subsequently the rude hut was made into a barn or pig-pen, and a respectable farmhouse was built; and finally this, too, has been replaced by a house of modern style and conveniences. If we could consider this change to have extended over thousands of years, from the first shelter of man to the finished modern building, it would be a picture of the progress of man in the art of building. In this slow process man struggled without means and with crude notions of life in every form. The aim, first, was for protection, then comfort and durability, and finally for beauty. The artistic in building has kept pace with other forms of civilization evinced in other ways.

One of the most interesting exhibits of house-building for protection is found in the cliff dwellings, whose ruins are to be seen in Arizona and New Mexico. Tradition and other evidences point to the conclusion that certain tribes had developed a state of civilization as high as a middle period of barbarism, on the plains, where they had made a beginning of systematic agriculture, and that they were afterward driven out by wilder tribes and withdrew, seeking the cliffs for protection. There they built under the projecting cliffs the large communal houses, where they dwelt for a long period of time. Subsequently their descendants went into the valleys and developed the Pueblo villages, with their large communal houses of *adobe*.

Discovery and Use of Metals.—It is not known just when the human race first discovered and used any one of the metals now known to commerce and industry, but it can be assumed that their discovery occurred at a very early period and their use followed quickly. Reasoning back from the nature and condition of the wild tribes of to-day, who are curiously attracted by bright colors, whether in metals or beads or clothing, and realizing how universally they used the minerals and plants for coloring, it would be safe to assume that the satisfaction of the curiosity of primitive man led to the discovery of bright metals at a very early time. Pieces of copper, gold, and iron would easily have been found in a free state in metal-bearing soil, and treasured as articles of value. Copper undoubtedly was used by the American Indians, and probably by the inhabitants of Europe during the Neolithic Age—it being found in a native state in sufficient quantities to be hammered into implements.

Thus copper has been found in large pieces in its native state, not only in Europe but in Mexico and other parts of North America, particularly in the Lake Superior region; but as the soft hematite iron was found in larger quantities in a free state, it would seem that the use of iron in a small degree must have occurred at about the same time, or perhaps a little later. The process of smelting must have been suggested by the action of fire built on or near ore beds, where a crude process of accidental smelting took place. Combined with tin ore, the copper was made into bronze in Peru and Mexico at the time of the discovery. In Europe there are abundant remains to show the early use of metals. Probably copper and tin were in use before iron, although iron may have been discovered first. There are numerous tin mines in Asia and copper mines in Cyprus. At first, metals were probably worked while cold through hammering, the softest metals doubtless being used before others.

It is difficult to tell how smelting was discovered, although the making and use of bronze implements is an indication of the first process of smelting ores and combining metals. When tin was first discovered is not known, but we know that bronze implements made from an alloy of copper, tin, and usually other metals were used by the Greeks and other Aryan peoples in the early historic period, about six thousand years ago. In Egypt and Babylon many of the inscriptions make mention of the use of iron as well as bronze, although the extended use of the former must have come about some time after the latter. At first all war instruments were stone and wood and later bronze, which were largely replaced by iron at a still later period. The making of spears, swords, pikes, battle-axes, and other implements of war had much to do with the development of ingenious work in metals. The final perfection of metal work could only be attained by the manufacture of finely treated steel. Probably the tempering of steel began at the time iron came prominently into use.

Other metals, such as silver, quicksilver, gold, and lead, came into common use in the early stages of civilization, all of which added greatly to the arts and industries. Nearly all of the metals were used for money at various times. The aids to trade and commerce which these metals gave on account of their universal use and constant measure of value cannot be overestimated.

Transportation as a Means of Economic Development.—Early methods of carrying goods from one place to another were on the backs of human beings. Many devices were made for economy of service and strength in carrying. Bands over the shoulders and over the head were devised for the purpose of securing the pack on the back. An Indian woman of the Southwest would carry a large basket, or *keiho*, on her back, secured by a band around her head for the support of the load. A Pueblo woman will carry a large bowl filled with water or other material, on the top of her head, balancing it by walking erect. Indeed, in more recent times washerwomen in Europe, and of the colored race in America, carry baskets of clothes and pails of water on their heads. The whole process of the development of transportation came about through invention to be relieved from this bodily service.

As the dog was the first animal domesticated, he was early used to help in transportation by harnessing him to a rude sled, or drag, by means of which he pulled articles from one place to another. The Eskimos have used dogs and the sled to a greater extent than any other race. The use of the camel, the llama, the horse, and the ass for packing became very common after their domestication. Huge packs were strapped upon the backs of these animals, and goods thus transported from one place to another. To such an extent was the camel used, even in the historic period, for transportation in the Orient that he has been called the "ship of the desert." The plains Indians had a method of attaching two poles, one at each side of an Indian pony, which extended backward, dragging on the ground. Upon these poles was built a little platform, on which goods were deposited and thus transported from one camp to another.

It must have been a long time before water transportation performed any considerable economic service. It is thought by some that primitive man conceived the idea of the use of water for transportation through his experience of floating logs, or drifts, or his own process of swimming and floating. Jack London pictures two primitives playing on the logs near the shore of a stream. Subsequently the logs cast loose, and the primitives were floated away from the shore. They learned by putting their hands in the water and paddling that they could make the logs move in the direction which they wished to go. Perhaps this explanation is as good as any, inasmuch as the beginnings of modern transportation still dwell in the mist of the past. However, in support of the log theory is the fact that modern races use primitive boats made of long reeds tied together, forming a loglike structure. The *balsa* of the Indians of the north coasts of South America is a very good representation of this kind of boat.

Evidently, the first canoes were made by hollowing logs and sharpening the ends at bow and stern. This form of boat-making has been carried to a high degree of skill by the Indians of the northwest coast of America and by the natives of the Hawaiian Islands. The birch-bark canoe, made for lighter work and overland transportation, is more suggestive of the light reed boat than of the log canoe. Also, the boats made of a framework covered with the skins of animals were prominent at certain periods of the development of races who lived on animal food. But later the development of boats with frames covered with strips of board and coated with pitch became the great vehicle of commerce through hundreds of years. It certainly is a long journey from the floating log to the modern floating passenger palace, freight leviathan, or armed dreadnought, but the journey was accomplished by thousands of steps, some short and some long, through thousands of years of progress.

Trade, or Exchange of Goods.—In Mr. Clark Wissler's book on *Man and Culture,* he has shown quite conclusively that there are certain culture areas whereby certain inventions, discoveries, or customs have originated and spread over a given territory. This recognition of a centre of origin of custom or invention is in accordance with the whole process of social development. For instance, in a given area occupied by modern civilized people, there are a very few who invent or originate things, and others follow through imitation or suggestion. So it was with the discoveries and inventions of primitive man. For example, we know that in Oklahoma and Arkansas, as well as in other places in the United States, certain stone quarries or mines are found that produce a certain kind of flint or chert used in making arrow-heads or spearheads and axes. Tribes that developed these traded with other tribes that did not have them, so that from these centres implements were scattered all over the West. A person may pick up on a single village site or battle-ground different implements coming from a dozen or more different quarries or centres and made by different tribes hundreds of miles apart in residence.

This diffusion of knowledge and things of material workmanship, or of methods of life, is through a system of borrowing, trading, or swapping—or perhaps sometimes through conquest and robbery; but as soon as an article of any kind could be made which could be subjected to general use of different tribes in different localities, it began to travel from a centre and to be used over a wide area. Certain tribes became special workers in specialized lines. Thus some were bead-makers, others expert tanners of hides, others makers of bows and arrows of peculiar quality, and others makers of stone implements. The incidental swapping of goods by tribes finally led to a systematic method of a travelling trader who brought goods from one tribe to another, exchanging as he went. This early trade had an effect in more rapid extension of culture, because in that case one tribe could have the invention, discovery, and art of all tribes. In connection with this is to be noted the slow change of custom regarding religious belief and ceremony or tribal consciousness. The pride of family and race development, the assumption of superiority leading to race aversion, interfered with intelligence and the spread of ideas and customs; but most economic processes that were not bound up with religious ceremonies or tribal customs were easily exchanged and readily accepted between the tribes.

Exchange of goods and transportation went hand in hand in their development, very slowly and surely. After trade had become pretty well established, it became necessary to have a medium of exchange. Some well-known article whose value was very well recognized among the people who were trading became the standard for fixing prices in exchange. Thus, in early Anglo-Saxon times the cow was the unit of the measure of value. Sometimes a shell, as a *cowrie* of India or the wampum of the American Indian, was used for this purpose. Wheat has been at one time in America, and tobacco in another, a measure of exchange because of the scarcity of money.

Gradually, as the discovery and use of precious metals became common and desirable because of their brightness and service in implement and ornament, they became the medium of exchange. Thus, copper and gold, iron and bronze have been used as metallic means of exchange—that is, as money. So from the beginning of trade and swapping article for article, it came to be common eventually to swap an article for something called money and then use the money for the purchase of other desirable articles. This made it possible for the individual to carry about in a small compass the means of obtaining any article in the market within the range of the purchasing power of his money. Trade, transportation, and exchange not only had a vast deal to do with economic progress but were of tremendous importance in social development. They were powerful in diffusion, extension, and promotion of culture.

The Struggle for Existence Develops the Individual and the Race.—The remnants and relics of the arts and industries of man give us a fair estimate of the process of man's mind and the accomplishment of his physical labor.

It is through the effort involved in the struggle for existence that he has made his various steps forward. Truly the actual life of primitive man tends to verify the adage that "necessity is the mother of invention." It was this tremendous demand on him for the means of existence that caused him to create the things that protected and improved his life. It was the insistent struggle which forced him to devise means of taking advantage of nature and thus led to invention and discovery. Every new invention and every new discovery showed the expansion of his mind, as well as gave him the means of material improvement. It also added to his bodily vigor and added much to the development of his physical powers. Upon this economic foundation has been built a superstructure of intellectual power, of moral worth and social improvement, for these in their highest phases of existence may be traced back to the early beginnings of life, where man was put to his utmost effort to supply the simplest of human wants.

SUBJECTS FOR FURTHER STUDY

1. The change in social life caused by the cultivation of the soil.

2. The effect of the discovery and use of fire on civilization.

3. What was the social effect of the exchange of economic products?

4. What influence had systematic labor on individual development?

5. Show how the discovery and use of a new food advances civilization.

6. Compare primitive man's food supply with that of a modern city dweller.

7. Trace a cup of coffee to its original source and show the different classes of people engaged in its production.

[1] *Man and Culture*.

[2] See Chapter III.

CHAPTER VI

PRIMITIVE SOCIAL LIFE

The Character of Primitive Social Life.—Judging from the cultures of prehistoric man in Europe and from analogies of living races that appear to have the same state of culture, strong inferences may be drawn as to the nature of the beginnings of human association. The hypothesis that man started as an individual and developed social life through mutual aid as he came in contact with his fellows does not cover the whole subject. It is not easy to conceive man in a state of isolation at any period of his life, but it appears true that his early associations were simple and limited to a few functions. The evidence of assemblage in caves, the kind of implements used, and the drawings on the walls of caves would appear to indicate that an early group life existed from the time of the first human cultures. The search for food caused men to locate at the same place. The number that could be supplied with food from natural subsistence in a given territory must have been small. Hence, it would appear that the early groups consisted of small bands. They moved on if the population encroached upon the food supply.

Also, the blood-related individuals formed the nucleus of the group. The dependency of the child on the mother led to the first permanent location as the seat of the home and the foundation of the family. As the family continued to develop and became the most permanent of all social institutions, it is easy to believe as a necessity that it had a very early existence. It came out of savagery into barbarism and became one of the principal bulwarks of civilization.

It may be accepted as a hypothesis that there was a time in the history of every branch of the human race when social order was indefinite and that out of this incoherence came by degrees a complex organized society. It was in such a rude state that the relations of individuals to each other were not clearly defined by custom, but were temporary and incidental. Family ties were loose and irregular, custom had not become fixed, law was unheard of, government was unknown unless it was a case of temporary leadership, and unity of purpose and reciprocal social life were wanting. Indeed, it is a picture of a human horde but little above the animal herd in its nature and composition. Living tribes such as the Fuegians and Australians, and the extinct Tasmanians, represent very nearly the status of the horde—a sort of social protoplasm. They wander in groups, incidentally through the influence of temporary advantage or on account of a fitful social instinct. Co-operation, mutual aid, and reciprocal mental action were so faint that in many cases life was practically non-social. Nevertheless, even these groups had aggregated, communicated, and had language and other evidences of social heredity.

The Family Is the Most Persistent of Social Origins.—The relation of parent and child was the most potent influence in establishing coherency of the group, and next to it, though of later development, was the relation of man and woman—that is, the sex relation. While the family is a universal social unit, it appears in many different forms in different tribes and, indeed, exhibits many changes in its development in the same tribe. There is no probability that mankind existed in a complete state of promiscuity in sex relations, yet these relations varied in different tribes. Mating was always a habit of the race and early became regulated by custom. The variety of forms of mating leads us to think the early sex life of man was not of a degraded nature. Granted that matrimony had not reached the high state of spiritual life contemplated in modern ideals, there are instances of monogamic marriage and pure, dignified rites in primitive peoples. Polygamy and polyandry were of later development.

A study of family life within the historic period, especially of Greeks, Romans, and Teutons, and possibly the Hebrews, compared with the family life of the Australian and some of the North American Indian tribes, reveals great contrasts in the prevailing customs of matrimony. All forms of marriage conceivable may be observed from rank animalism to high spiritual union; of numerous ideals, customs, and usages and ceremonies, as well as great confusion of purpose. It may be assumed, therefore, that there was a time in the history of every branch of the human race when family customs were indefinite and family coherence was lacking. Also that society was in a rude state in which the relations of individuals to each other and to the general social group were not clearly defined. There are found to-day among the lower races, in the Pacific islands, Africa, and South America, evidences of lack of cohesive life. They represent groups of people without permanent organization, held together by temporary advantage, with crude, purposeless customs, with the exercise of fitful social instinct.

However, it is out of such conditions that the tribes, races, and nations of the early historic period have evolved into barbaric organization. Reasoning backward by the comparative method, one may trace the survivals of ancient customs. Following the social heredity of the oldest civilized tribes, such as the Egyptians, Babylonians, Greeks, Romans, and Teutonic peoples, there is evidence of the rise from a rude state of savagery to a higher social life. Historical records indicate the passage from the middle state of barbarism to advanced civil life, even though the earlier phases of social life of primitive man remain obscure. The study of tradition and a comparison of customs and language of races yield a definite knowledge of the evolution of society.

Kinship Is a Strong Factor in Social Organization.—Of all causes that held people in coherent union, perhaps kinship, natural and artificial, was the most potent. All of the direct and indirect offspring of a single pair settled in the same family group. This enlarged family took its place as the only organ of social order. Not only did all the relatives settle and become members of one body, but also strangers who needed protection were admitted to the family by subscribing to their customs and religion. Thus the father of the family had a numerous following, composed of relatives by birth and by adoption. He was the ruler of this enlarged household, declaring the customs of his fathers, leading the armed men in war, directing the control of property, for he alone was the owner of all their possessions, acting as priest in the administration of religious ceremonies—a service performed only by him—and acting as judge in matters of dispute or discipline. Thus the family was a compact organization with a central authority, in which both chief and people were bound by custom.

Individuals were born under status and must submit to whatever was customary in the rule of the family or tribe. There was no law other than custom to determine the relation of individuals to one another. Each must abide in the sphere of activity into which he was born. He could not rise above it, but must submit to the arbitrary rule of traditional usage. The only position an individual had was in the family, and he must observe what custom had taught. This made family life arbitrary and conventional.

The Earliest Form of Social Order.—The family is sometimes called the unit of society. The best historical records of the family are found in the Aryan people, such as the Greeks, the Romans, and the Teutons. Outside of this there are many historical references to the Aryans in their primitive home in Asia, and the story of the Hebrew people, a branch of the Semitic race, shows many phases of tribal and family life. The ancient family differed from the modern in organization and composition. The first historical family was the patriarchal, by which we mean a family group in which descent was traced in the male line, and in which authority was vested in the eldest living male inhabitant. It is held by some that this is the original family type, and that the forms which we find among savage races are degenerate forms of the above. Some have advocated that the patriarchal family was the developed form of the family, and only occurred after a long evolution through states of promiscuity, polygamy, and polyandry. There is much evidence that the latter assumption is true. But there is evidence that the patriarchal family was the first political unit of all the Aryan races, and also of the Semitic as well, and that monogamic marriage was developed in these ancient societies so far as historical evidence can determine. The ancient Aryans in their old home, those who came into India, Greece, Rome, and the northern countries of Europe, whether Celt or Teuton, all give evidence of the permanency of early family organization.

The Reign of Custom.—For a long period custom reigned supreme, and arbitrary social life became conventionalized, and the change from precedent became more and more difficult. The family was despotic, exacting, unyielding in its nature, and individual activity was absorbed in it. So powerful was this early sway of customary law that many tribes never freed themselves from its bondage. Others by degrees slowly evolved from its crystallizing influences. Changes in custom came about largely through the migration of tribes, which brought new scenes and new conditions, the intercourse of one tribe with another in trade and war, and the gradual shifting of the internal life of the social unit. Those tribes that were isolated were left behind in the progress of the race, and to many of them still clung the customs practised thousands of years before. Those that went forward from this first status grew by practice rather than by change of ideals. It is the law of all progress that ideals are conservative, and that they can be broken away from only by the procedure of actual practice. Gradually the reign of customary law gave way to the laws framed by the people. The family government gave way to the political; the individual eventually became the political unit, and freedom of action prevailed in the entire social body.

The Greek and Roman Family Was Strongly Organized.—In Greece and Rome the family enlarged and formed the gens, the gentes united into a tribe, and the tribe passed into the nation. In all of this formulated government the individual was represented by his family and received no recognition except as a member of such. The tribal chief became the king, or, as he is sometimes called, the patriarchal president, because he presided over a band of equals in power, namely, the assembled elders of the tribe. The heads of noble families were called together to consider the affairs of government, and at a common meal the affairs of the nation were discussed over viands and wine. The king thus gathered the elders about him for the purpose of considering measures to be laid before the people. The popular assembly, composed of all the citizens, was called to sanction what the king and the elders had decreed. Slowly the binding forms of traditional usage were broken down, and the king and his people were permitted to enact those laws which best served the immediate ends of government. True, the old formal life of the family continued to exist. There were the gentes, tribes, and phratries, or brotherhoods, that still existed, and the individual entered the state in civil capacity through his family. But by degrees the old family régime gave way to the new political life, and sovereign power was vested in monarchy, democracy, or aristocracy, according to the nature of the sovereignty.

The functions or activities and powers of governments, which were formerly vested in the patriarchal chief, or king, and later in king, people, and council, gradually became separated and were delegated to different authorities, though the sharp division of legislative, judicial, and executive functions which characterizes our modern governments did not exist. These forms of government were more or less blended, and it required centuries to distribute the various powers of government into special departments and develop modern forms.

In Primitive Society Religion Occupied a Prominent Place.—While kinship was first in order in the foundation of units of social organization, religion was second to it in importance. Indeed, it is considered by able writers as the foundation of the family and, as the ethnic state is but the expanded family, the vital power in the formation of the state. Among the Aryan tribes religion was a prominent feature of association. In the Greek household stood the family altar, resting upon the first soil in possession of the family. Only members of the household could worship at this shrine, and only the eldest male members of the family in good standing could conduct religious service. When the family grew into the gens it also had a separate altar and a separate worship. Likewise, the tribe had its own worship, and when the city was formed it had its own temple and a particular deity, whom the citizens worshipped. In the ancient family the worship of the house spirit or a deified ancestor was the common practice. This practice of the worship of departed heroes and ancestors, which prevailed in all of the various departments of old Greek society, tended to develop unity and purity of family and tribe. As family forms passed into political, the religion changed from a family to a national religion.

Among the lower tribes the religious life is still most powerful in influencing their early life. Mr. Tylor, in his valuable work on *Primitive Culture*, has devoted a good part of two large volumes to the treatment of early religious belief. While recognizing that there is no complete definition of religion, he holds that "belief in spiritual beings" is a minimum definition which will apply to all religions, and, indeed, about the only one that will. The lower races each had simple notions of the spiritual world. They believed in a soul and its existence after death. Nearly all believed in both good and evil spirits, and in one or more greater gods or spirits who ruled and managed the universe. In this early stage of religious belief philosophy and religion were one. The belief in the after life of the spirit is evidenced by implements which were placed in the grave for the use of the departed, and by food which was placed at the grave for his subsistence on the journey. Indeed, some even set aside food at each meal for the departed; others, as instanced by the Greeks, placed tables in the burying ground for the dead. Many views were entertained by the early people concerning the origin of the soul and its course after death. But in all of the rude conditions of life religion was indefinite and uncultured. From lower simple forms it arose to more complex systems and to higher generalizations.

Religious influence on progress has been very great. There are those who have neglected the subject of religion in the discussion of the history of civilization. Other writers have considered it of little importance, and still others believe it to have been a positive hindrance to the development of the race. Religion, in general, as practised by savage and barbarous races, based, as it is largely, on superstition, must of a necessity be conservative and non-progressive. Yet the service which it performs in making the tribe or family cohesive and in giving an impetus to the development of the mind before the introduction of science and art as special studies is, indeed, great. The early forms of culture are found almost wholly in religious belief and practice.

The religious ceremonies at the grave of a departed companion, around the family altar or in the congregation, whether in the temple or in the open air, tended to social cohesion and social activity. The exercise of religious belief in a superior being and a recognition of his authority, had a tendency to bring the actions of individuals into orderly arrangement and to develop unity of life. It also had a strong tendency to prepare the simple mind of the primitive man for later intellectual development. It gave the mind something to contemplate, something to reason about, before it reached a stage of scientific investigation. Its moral influence is unquestioned. While some of the early religions are barbarous in the extreme in their degenerate state, as a whole they teach man to consider himself and his fellows, and develop an ethical relationship. And while altruism as a great factor in religious and in social progress appeared at a comparatively recent period, it has been in existence from the earliest associations of men to the present time, and usually makes its strongest appeal through religious belief. Religion thus becomes a great society-builder, as well as a means of individual culture.

Spirit Worship.—The recognition of the continued journey of the spirit after death was in itself an altruistic practice. Much of the worship of the controlling spirit was conducted to secure especial favor to the departed soul. The burial service in early religious practice became a central idea in permanent religious rites. Perhaps the earliest phase of religious belief arises out of the idea that the spirit or soul of man has control over the body. It gives rise to the notion of spirit and the idea of continued existence. Considering the universe as material existence, according to primitive belief, it is the working of the superior spirit over the physical elements that gives rise to natural phenomena.

One of the early stages of religious progress is to attempt to form a meeting-place with the spirit. This desire is seen in the lowest tribes and in the highest civilization of to-day. When Cabrillo came to the coast of southern California he found natives that had never before come in contact with civilized people. He describes a rude temple made by driving stakes in the ground in a circular form, and partitioning the enclosure by similar rows of stakes. At the centre was a rude platform, on which were placed the feathers of certain birds pleasing to the spirit. The natives came to this temple occasionally, and, circling around it, went through many antics of worship. This represents the primitive idea of location in worship. Not different in its fundamental conception from the rude altar of stones built by Abraham at Bethel, the Greek altar, or the mighty columns of St. Peter's, it was the simple meeting-place of man and the spirit. For all of these represent location in worship, and just as the modern worshipper enters the church or cathedral to meet God, so did the primitive savage fix locations for the meeting of the spirit.

Man finally attempted to control the spirit for his own advantage. A rude form of religion was reached, found in certain stages of the development of all religions, in which man sought to manipulate or exorcise the spirits who existed in the air or were located in trees, stones, and other material forms. Out of this came a genuine worship of the powerful, and supplication for help and support. Seeking aid and favor became the fundamental ideas in religious worship. Simple in the beginning, it sought to appease the wrath of the evil spirit and gain the favor of the good. But finally it sought to worship on account of the sublimity and power possessed by the object of worship. With the advancement of religious practice, religious beliefs and religious ceremonies became more complex. Great systems of mythology sprang up among nations about to enter the precincts of civilization, and polytheism predominated. Purely ethical religions were of a later development, for the notion of the will of the gods concerning the treatment of man by his fellows belongs to an advanced stage of religious belief. The ethical importance of religion reaches its culmination in the religion of Jesus Christ.

Moral Conditions.—The slow development of altruistic notions presages a deficiency of moral action in the early stages of human progress. True it is that moral conditions seem never to be entirely wanting in this early period. There are many conflicting accounts of the moral practice of different savage and barbarous tribes when first discovered by civilized man. Tribes differ much in this respect, and travellers have seen them from different standpoints. Wherever a definite moral practice cannot be observed, it may be assumed that the standard is very low. Moral progress seems to consist in the constantly shifting standards of right and wrong, of justice and injustice. Perhaps the moral action of the savage should be viewed from two standpoints—namely, the position of the average savage of the tribe, and from the vantage of modern ethical standards. It is only by considering it from these two views that we have the true estimation of his moral status. There must be a difference between conventionality and morality, and many who have judged the moral status of the savage have done so more from a conventional than from a moral standard. True that morality must be judged from the individual motive and from social effects of individual action. Hence it is that the observance of conventional rules must be a phase of morality; yet it is not all of morality. Where conventionality does not exist, the motive of action must be the true moral test.

The actions of some savages and of barbarous people are revolting in the extreme, and so devoid of sympathy for the sufferings of their fellow-beings as to lead us to assume that they are entirely without moral sentiment. The repulsive spectacle of human sacrifice is frequently brought about by religious fervor, while the people have more or less altruistic practice in other ways. This practice was common to very many tribes, and indeed to some nations entering the pale of civilization. Cannibalism, revolting as it may seem, may be practised by a group of people which, in every other respect, shows moral qualities. It is composed of kind husbands, mothers, brothers, and sisters, who look after each other's welfare. The treatment of infants, not only by savage tribes but by the Greek and Roman nations after their entrance into civilized life, represents a low status of morality, for it was the common custom to expose infants, even in these proud nations. The degraded condition of woman, as slave and tool of man in the savage state, and indeed in the ancient civilization, does not speak well for the high standard of morality of the past. More than this, the disregard of the rights of property and person and the common practice of revolting brutality, are conclusive evidence of the low moral status of early mankind.

Speaking of the Sioux Indians, a writer says: "They regard most of the vices as virtues. Theft, arson, rape, and murder are among them regarded with distinction, and the young Indian from childhood is taught to regard killing as the highest of virtues." And a writer who had spent many years among the natives of the Pacific coast said that "whatever is falsehood in the European is truth in the Indian, and vice versa." Whether we consider the savages or barbarians of modern times, or the ancient nations that laid claim to civilization, we find a gradual evolution of the moral practice and a gradual change of the standard of right. This standard has constantly advanced until it rests to-day on the Golden Rule and other altruistic principles of Christian teaching.

Warfare and Social Progress.—The constant warfare of savages and barbarians was not without its effects in developing the individual and social life. Cruel and objectionable as it is, the study and practice of war was an element of strength. It developed physical courage, and taught man to endure suffering and hardships. It developed intellectual power in the struggle to circumvent and overcome enemies. It led to the device and construction of arms, machines, engines, guns, and bridges, for facilitating the carrying on of successful warfare; all of this was instrumental in developing the inventive genius and engineering skill of man.

In a political way warfare developed tribal or national unity, and bound more closely together the different groups in sympathy and common interest. It thus became useful in the preparation for successful civil government. It prepared some to rule and others to obey, and divided the governing from the governed, an essential characteristic of all forms of government. Military organization frequently accompanied or preceded the formation of the modern state. Sparta and Rome, and in more modern times Prussia, were built upon military foundations.

The effect of war in depopulating countries has proved a detriment to civilization by disturbing economic and social development and by destroying thousands of lives. Looking back over the track which the human race has made in its persistent advance, it is easy to see that the ravages of war are terrible. While ethical considerations have entered into warfare and made its effects less terrible, it still is deplorable. It is not a necessity to modern civilization for the development of intellectual or physical strength, nor for the development of either patriotism or courage. Modern warfare is a relic of barbarism, and the sooner we can avoid it the better. Social progress means the checking of war in every way and the development of the arts of peace. It is high time that the ethical process between nations should take the place of the art of war.

Mutual Aid Developed Slowly.—Owing to ignorance and to the instinct for self-preservation, man starts on his journey toward progress on an individualistic and selfish basis. Gradually he learns to associate with his fellows on a co-operative basis. The elements which enter into this formal association are the exercise of a general blood relationship, religion, economic life, social and political organization. With the development of each of these, social order progresses. Yet, in the clashing interests of individuals and tribes, in the clumsy methods adopted in the mastery of nature, what a waste of human energy; what a loss of human life! How long it has taken mankind to associate on rational principles, to develop a pure home life, to bring about toleration in religion, to develop economic co-operation, to establish liberality in government, and to promote equality and justice! By the rude master, experience, has man been taught all this at an immense cost. Yet there was no other way possible.

SUBJECTS FOR FURTHER STUDY

1. Study your community to determine that society is formed by the interactions of individuals.

2. Discuss the earliest forms of mutual aid.

3. Why is the family called the unit of social organization?

4. Why did religion occupy such an important place in primitive society?

5. To what extent and in what manner did the patriarchal family take the place of the state?

6. What is the relation of morals to religion?

7. What are the primary social groups? What the secondary?

CHAPTER VII

LANGUAGE AND ART AS A MEANS OF CULTURE AND SOCIAL DEVELOPMENT

The Origin of Language Has Been a Subject of Controversy.—Since man began to philosophize on the causes of things, tribes and races and, indeed, philosophers of all times have attempted to determine the origin of language and to define its nature. In early times language was a mystery, and for lack of better explanation it was frequently attributed to the direct gift of the Deity. The ancient Aryans deified language, and represented it by a goddess "which rushes onward like the wind, which bursts through heaven and earth, and, awe-inspiring to each one that it loves, makes him a Brahmin, a poet, and a sage." Men used language many centuries before they seriously began to inquire into its origin and structure. The ancient Hindu philosophers, the Greeks, and all early nations that had begun a speculative philosophy, wonderingly tried to ascertain whence language came. Modern philologists have carried their researches so far as to ascertain with tolerable accuracy the history and life of language and to determine with the help of other scientists the facts and phenomena of its origin.

Language, in its broadest sense, includes any form of expression by which thoughts and feelings are communicated from one individual to another. Words may be spoken, gestures made, cries uttered, pictures or characters drawn, or letters made as means of expression. The deaf-mute converses with his fingers and his lips; the savage communicates by means of gesticulation. It is easy to conceive of a community in which all communication is carried on in sign language. It is said that the Grebos of Africa carry this mode of expression to such an extent that the persons and tenses of the mood are indicated with the hands alone.

It has been advocated by some that man first learned to talk by imitating the sounds of nature. It is sometimes called the "bow-wow" theory of the origin of language. Words are used to express the meaning of nature. Thus the purling of the brook, the lowing of the cow, the barking of the dog, the moaning of the wind, the rushing of water, the cry of animals, and other expressions of nature were imitated, and thus formed the root words of language. This theory was very commonly upheld by the philosophers of the eighteenth century, but is now regarded as an entirely inadequate explanation of the process of the development of language. It is true that every language has words formed by the imitation of sound, but these are comparatively few, and as languages are traced toward their origin, such words seem to have continually less importance. Nothing conclusive has been proved concerning the origin of any language by adopting this theory.

Another theory is that the exclamations and interjections suddenly made have been the formation of root words, which in turn give rise to the complex forms of language. This can scarcely be considered of much force, for the difference between sudden explosive utterance and words expressing full ideas is so great as to be of little value in determining the real formation of language. These sudden interjections are more of the nature of gesture than of real speech.

The theologians insisted for many years that language was a gift of God, but failed to show how man could learn the language after it was given him. They tried to show that man was created with his full powers of speech, thought, and action, and that a vocabulary was given him to use on the supposition that he would know how to use it. But, in fact, nothing yet has been proved concerning the first beginnings of language. There is no reason why man should be fully equipped in language any more than in intellect, moral quality, or economic condition, and it is shown conclusively that in all these characteristics he has made a slow evolution. Likewise the further back towards its origin we trace any language or any group of languages the simpler we find it, coming nearer and yet nearer to the root speech. If we could have the whole record of man, back through that period into which historical records cannot go, and into which comparative philology throws but a few rays of light, doubtless we should find that at one time man used gesture, facial expression, and signs, interspersed with sounds at intervals, as his chief means of expression. Upon this foundation mankind has built the superstructure of language.

Some philosophers hold that the first words used were names applied to familiar objects. Around these first names clustered ideas, and gradually new words appeared. With the names and gestures it was easy to convey thought. Others, refuting this idea, have held that the first words represented general notions and not names. From these general notions there were gradually instituted the specific words representing separate ideas. Others have held that language is a gift, and springs spontaneously in the nature of man, arising from his own inherent qualities. Possibly from different standpoints there is a grain of truth in each one of these theories, although all combined are insufficient to explain the whole truth.

No theory yet devised answers all the questions concerning the origin of language. It may be truly asserted that language is an acquisition, starting with the original capacity for imperfect speech found in the physiological structure of man. This is accompanied by certain tendencies of thought and life which furnish the psychical notion of language-formation. These represent the foundations of language, and upon this, through action and experience, the superstructure of language has been built. There has been a continuous evolution from simple to complex forms.

Language Is an Important Social Function.—Whatever conjectures may be made by philosophers or definite knowledge determined by philologists, it is certain that language has been built up by human association. Granted that the physiological function of speech was a characteristic of the first beings to bear the human form, it is true that its development has come about by the mental interactions of individuals. No matter to what extent language was used by a given generation, it was handed on through social heredity to the next generation. Thus, language represents a continuous stream of word-bearing thought, moving from the beginning of human association to the present time. It is through it that we have a knowledge of the past and frame the thoughts of the present. While it is easy to concede that language was built up in the attempt of man to communicate his feelings, emotions, and thoughts to others, it in turn has been a powerful coercive influence and a direct social creation. Only those people who could understand one another could be brought into close relationships, and for this purpose some generally accepted system of communicating ideas became essential. Moreover, the tribes and assimilated nations found the force of common language in the coherency of group life. Thus it became a powerful instrument in developing tribal, racial, or national independence. If the primal force of early family or tribal organization was that of sex and blood relationship, language became a most powerful ally in forcing the group into formal social action, and in furnishing a means of defense against the social encroachments of other tribes and nations.

It must be observed, however, that the social boundaries of races are not coincident with the divisions of language. In general the tendency is for a race to develop an independent language, for racial development was dependent upon isolation from other groups. But from the very earliest associations to the present time there has been a tendency for assimilation of groups even to the extent of direct amalgamation of those occupying contiguous territory, or through conquest. In the latter event, the conquered group usually took the language of the conquerors, although this has not always followed, as eventually the stronger language becomes the more important through use. For instance, for a time after the Norman Conquest, Norman French became, in the centres of government and culture at least, the dominant language, but eventually was thrown aside by a more useful language as English institutions came to the front. As race and language may not represent identical groups, it is evident that a classification of language cannot be taken as conclusive evidence in the classification of races. However, in the main it is true. A classification of all of the languages of the Indians of North America would be a classification of all the tribes that have been differentiated in physical structure and other racial traits, as well as of habits and customs. Yet a tribe using a common language may be composed of a number of racial elements.

When it comes to the modern state, language does not coincide with natural boundaries. Thus, in Switzerland German is spoken in the north and northeast, French in the southwest, and Italian in the southeast. However, in this case, German is the dominant language taught in schools and used largely in literature. Also, in Belgium, where one part of the people speak Flemish and the other French, they are living under the same national unity so far as government is concerned, although there have always remained distinctive racial types. In Mexico there are a number of tribes that, though using the dominant Spanish language, called Mexican, are in their closer associations speaking the primitive languages of their race or tribe which have come down to them through long ages of development. Sometimes, however, a tribe shows to be a mosaic of racial traits and languages, brought about by the complete amalgamation of tribes. A very good example of this complete amalgamation would be that of the Hopi Indians of New Mexico, where distinctive group words and racial traits may be traced to three different tribes. But to refer to a more complete civilization, where the Spanish language is spoken in Spain, we find the elements of Latin, Teutonic, Arabic, and Old Iberian speech, which are suggestive of different racial traits pointing to different racial origins.

Regardless of origin and tradition, language gradually conforms to the type of civilization in existence. A strong, vigorous industrial nation would through a period of years develop a tendency for a vigorous language which would express the spirit and life of the people, while a dreamy, conservative nation would find little change in the language. Likewise, periods of romance or of war have a tendency to make changes in the form of speech in conformity to ideals of life. On the other hand, social and intellectual progress is frequently dependent upon the character of the language used to the extent that it may be said that language is an indication of the progress of a people in the arts of civilized life. It is evident in comparing the Chinese language with the French, great contrasts are shown in the ease in which ideas are represented and the stream of thought borne on its way. The Chinese language is a clumsy machine as compared with the flexible and smooth-gliding French. It appears that if it were possible for the Chinese to change their language for a more flexible, smooth-running instrument, it would greatly facilitate their progress in art, science, and social life.

Written Language Followed Speech in Order of Development.—Many centuries elapsed before any systematic writing or engraving recorded human events. The deeds of the past were handed on through tradition, in the cave, around the campfire, and in the primitive family. Stories of the past, being rehearsed over and over, became a permanent heritage, passing on from generation to generation. But this method of descent of knowledge was very indefinite, because story-tellers, influenced by their environment, continually built the present into the past, and so the truth was not clearly expressed.

Slowly man began to make a permanent record of deeds and events, the first beginnings of which were very feeble, and were included in drawings on the walls of caves, inscriptions on bone, stone, and ivory, and symbols woven in garments. All represented the first beginnings of the representative art of language.

Gradually picture-writing became so systematized that an expression of continuous thought might be recorded and transferred from one to another through the observation of the symbols universally recognized. But these pictures on rocks and ivory, and later on tablets, have been preserved, and are expressive of the first steps of man in the art of written language. The picture-writing so common to savages and barbarians finally passes from a simple *rebus* to a very complex written language, as in the case of the Egyptian or Mexican. The North American Indians used picture-writing in describing battles, or an expedition across a lake, or an army on a march, or a buffalo hunt. A simple picture shows that fifty-one warriors, led by a chief and his assistant, in five canoes, took three days to cross a lake and land their forces on the other side.

The use of pictographs is the next step in the process of written language. It represents a generalized form of symbols which may be put together in such a way as to express complete thoughts. Originally they were merely symbols or signs of ideas, which by being slightly changed in form or position led to the expression of a complete thought.

Following the pictograph is the ideograph, which is but one more step in the progress of systematic writing. Here the symbol has become so generalized that it has a significance quite independent of its origin. In other words, it becomes idealized and conventionalized, so that a specific symbol stood for a universal idea. It could be made specific by changing its form or position. All that was necessary now was to have a sufficient number of general symbols representing ideas, to build up a constructive language. The American Indian and the Chinese have apparently passed through all stages of the picture-writing, the use of the pictograph and of the ideograph. In fact, the Chinese language is but an extension of these three methods of expression. The objects were originally designated by a rude drawing, and then, to modify the meaning, different characters were attached to the picture. Thus a monosyllabic language was built up, and the root word had many meanings by the modification of its form and sometimes by the change of its position. The hieroglyphic writings of the Egyptians, Moabites, Persians, and Assyrians went through these methods of language development, as their records show to this day.

Phonetic Writing Was a Step in Advance of the Ideograph.—The difference between the phonetic writing and the picture-writing rests in the fact that the symbol representing the object is expressive of an idea or a complete thought, while in phonetic writing the symbol represents a sound which combined with other sounds expresses an idea called a word and complete thoughts through combination of words. The discovery and use of a phonetic alphabet represent the key to modern civilization. The invention of writing elevated man from a state of barbarism to a state of civilization. About the tenth century before Christ the Phoenicians, Hebrews, and other allied Semitic races began to use the alphabet. Each letter was named from a word beginning with it. The Greeks learned the alphabet from the Phoenicians, and the Greeks, in turn, passed it to the Romans. The alphabet continually changed from time to time. The old Phoenician was weak in vowel sounds, but the defect was remedied in the Greek and Roman alphabets and in the alphabets of the Teutonic nations. Fully equipped with written and spoken speech, the nations of the world were prepared for the interchange of thought and ideas and for the preservation of knowledge in an accurate manner. History could be recorded, laws written and preserved, and the beginnings of science elaborated.

The Use of Manuscripts and Books Made Permanent Records.—At first all records were made by pen, pencil, or stylus, and manuscripts were represented on papyrus paper or parchment, and could only be duplicated by copying. In Alexandria before the Christian era one could buy a copy of the manuscript of a great author, but it was at a high price. It finally became customary for monks, in their secluded retreats, to spend a good part of their lives in copying and preserving the manuscript writings of great authors. But it was not until printing was invented that the world of letters rapidly moved forward. Probably about the sixth century A.D. the Chinese began to print a group of characters from blocks, and by the tenth century they were engaged in keeping their records in this way. Gutenberg, Faust, and others improved upon the Chinese method by a system of movable type. But what a wonderful change since the fourteenth century printing! Now, with modern type-machines, fine grades of paper made by improved machinery, and the use of immense steam presses, the making of an ordinary book is very little trouble. Looking back over the course of events incident to the development of the modern complex and flexible language we observe, first, the rude picture scrawled on horn or rock. This was followed by the representation of the sound of the name of the picture, which passed into the mere sound sign. Finally, the relation between the figure and the sound becomes so arbitrary that the child learns the a, b, c as pure signs representing sounds which, in combination, make words which stand for ideas.

Language Is an Instrument of Culture.—Culture areas always spread beyond the territory of language groups. Culture depends upon the discovery and utilization of the forces of nature through invention and adaptation. It may spread through imitation over very large human territory. Man has universal mental traits, with certain powers and capacities that are developed in a relative order and in a degree of efficiency; but there are many languages and many civilizations of high and low degree. Through human speech the life of the past may be handed on to others and the life of the present communicated to one another. The physiological power of speech which exists in all permits every human group to develop a language in accordance with its needs and as influenced by its environment. Thus language advanced very rapidly as an instrument of communication even at a very early period of cultural development. A recent study of the languages of the American Indians has shown the high degree of the art of expression among people of the Neolithic culture. This would seem to indicate that primitive peoples are more definite in thought and more observant in the relation of cause and effect than is usually supposed. Thus, definite language permits more precise thought, and definite thought, in turn, insists on more exact expression in language. The two aid each other in development of cultural ideas, and invention and language move along together in the development of the human race. It becomes a great human invention, and as such it not only preserves the thoughts of the past but unlocks the knowledge of the present.

Not only is language the means of communication, and the great racial as well as social bond of union, but it represents knowledge, culture, and refinement. The strength and beauty of genuine artistic expression have an elevating influence on human life and become a means of social progress. The drama and the choicest forms of prose and poetry in their literary aspects furnish means of presenting great thoughts and high ideals, and, thus combined with the beauty of expression, not only furnish the best evidence of moral and intellectual progress but make a perennial source of information in modern social life. Hence it is that language and culture in all of their forms go hand in hand so closely that a high degree of culture is not attained without a dignified and expressive language.

Art as a Language of Aesthetic Ideas.—The development of aesthetic ideas and aesthetic representations has kept pace with progress in other phases of civilization. The notion of beauty as entertained by the savage is crude, and its representation is grotesque. Its first expression is observed in the adornment of the body, either by paint, tattooing, or by ornaments. The coarse, glaring colors placed upon the face or body, with no regard for the harmony of color, may attract attention, but has little expression of beauty from a modern standard. The first adornment in many savage tribes consisted in tattooing the body, an art which was finally rendered useless after clothing was fully adopted, except as a totemic design representing the unity of the tribe. This custom was followed by the use of rude jewelry for arms, neck, ears, nose, or lips. Other objects of clothing and ornament were added from time to time, the bright colors nearly always prevailing. There must have been in all tribes a certain standard of artistic taste, yet so low in many instances as to suggest only the grotesque. The taste displayed in the costumes of savages within the range of our own observation is remarkable for its variety. It ranges all the way from a small piece of cloth to the elaborate robes made of highly colored cotton and woollen goods. The Celts were noted for their highly colored garments and the artistic arrangement of the same. The Greeks displayed a grace and simplicity in dress never yet surpassed by any other nation. Yet the dress of early Greeks, Romans, and Teutons was meagre in comparison with modern elaborate costumes. All of this is a method of expression of the emotions and ideas and, in one sense, is a language of the aesthetic.

Representative art, even among primitive peoples, carries with it a distinctive language. It is a representation of ideas, as well as an attempt at beauty of expression. The figures on pottery and basketry frequently carry with them religious ideas for the expression and perpetuation of religious emotion and belief. Even rude drawings attempt to record the history of the deeds of the race. Progress is shown in better lines, in better form, and a more exquisite blending of colors. That many primitive people display a high degree of art and a low degree of general culture is one of the insoluble problems of the race. Perhaps it may be attributed primarily to the fact that all artistic expression originally sprang from the emotional side of life, and, in addition, may be in part attributed to the early training in the acute observation of the forms of nature by primitive people upon which depended their existence.

Music Is a Form of Language.—Early poetry was a recital of deeds, and a monotonous chant, which finally became recorded as language developed. The sagas and the war songs were the earliest expressions which later were combined with dramatic action. The poetry of primitive races has no distinguishing characteristics except metre or rhythm. It is usually an oft-recurring expression of the same idea. Yet there are many fragmentary examples of lyric poetry, though it is mostly egoistic, the individual reciting his deeds or his desires. From the natives of Greenland we have the following about the hovering of the clouds about the mountain:

> "The great Koonak mountain, over there—
> I see it;
> The great Koonak mountain, over there—
> I am looking at it;
> The bright shining in the South, over there—
> I admire it;
> The other side of Koonak—
> It stretches out—
> That which Koonak—
> Seaward encloses.
> See how they in the South
> Move and change—
> See how in the South
> They beautify one another;
> While it toward the sea
> Is veiled—by changing clouds
> Veiled toward the sea
> Beautifying one another."

The emotional nature of savages varies greatly in different tribes. The lives of some seem to be moved wholly through the emotions, while others are stolid or dull. The variations in musical ability and practice of savage and barbarous races are good evidence of this. Many of the tribes in Africa have their rude musical instruments, and chant their simple, monotonous music. The South Sea Islanders beat hollow logs with clubs, marking time and creating melody by these notes. The Dahomans use a reed fife, on which they play music of several notes. In all primitive music, time is the chief element, and this is not always kept with any degree of accuracy. The chanting of war songs, the moaning of the funeral dirge, or the sprightly singing with the dance, shows the varied expression of the emotional nature.

No better illustration of the arts of pleasure may be observed than the practices of the Zuñi Indians and other Pueblo Indians of New Mexico. The Zuñi melodies are sung on various festival occasions. Some are sacred melodies, used in worship; others are on the occasion of the celebration of the rabbit hunt, the rain dances, and the corn dances. Among the Pueblo Indians the cachina dance is for the purpose of invoking bountiful rains and good harvests. In all of their feasts, games, plays, and dances there are connected ceremonies of a religious nature. Religion occupies a very strong position in the minds of the people. Possessed of a superstitious nature, it was inevitable that all the arts of pleasure should partake somewhat of the religious ceremony. The song and the dance and the beating of the drums always accompanied every festival.

The Dance as a Means of Dramatic Expression.—Among primitive peoples the dance, poetry, and music were generally introduced together, and were parts of one drama. As such it was a social institution, with the religious, war, or play element fully represented. Most primitive dances were conducted by men only. In the celebrated *Corroboree* of the Australians, men danced and the women formed the orchestra.[1] This gymnastic dance was common to many tribes. The dances of the Moros and Igorrotes at the St. Louis Exposition partook, in a similar way, of the nature of the gymnastic dance. The war dances of the plains Indians of America are celebrated for their grotesqueness. The green-corn dance and the cachina of the Pueblos and the snake dance of the Moqui all have an economic foundation. In all, however, the play element in man and the desire for dramatic expression and the art of mimicry are evident. The chief feature of the dance of the primitive people is the regular time beat. This is more prominent than the grace of movement. Yet this agrees with the nature of their music, for in this the time element is more prominent than the tune. Rhythm is the strong element in the primitive art of poetry, music, or the dance, but all have an immense socializing influence. The modern dance has added to rhythm the grace of expression and developed the social tendencies. In it love is a more prominent feature than war or religion.

Catlin, in his *North American Indians*, describes the buffalo dance of the Mandan Indians, which appears to be more of a service toward an economic end than an art of pleasure. After an unsuccessful hunt the returned warriors bring out their buffalo masks, made of the head and horns and tail of the buffalo. These they don, and continue to dance until worn out. Ten or fifteen dancers form a ring and, accompanied by drumming, yelling, and rattling, dance until the first exhausted one goes through the pantomime of being shot with the bow and arrow, skinned, and cut up; but the dance does not lag, for another masked dancer takes the place of the fallen one. The dance continues day and night, without cessation, sometimes for two or three weeks, or until a herd of buffaloes appears in sight; then the warriors change the dance for the hunt.

The dancing of people of lower culture was carried on in many instances to express feelings and wishes. Many of the dances of Egypt, Greece, and other early civilizations were of this nature. Sacred hymns to the gods were chanted in connection with the dancing; but the sacred dance has become obsolete, in Western civilization its place being taken by modern church music.

The Fine Arts Follow the Development of Language.—While art varied in different tribes, we may assume in general that there was a continuity of culture development from the rude clay idol of primitive folk to the Venus de Milo or the Winged Victory; from the pictures on rocks and in caves to the Sistine Madonna; from the uncouth cooking bowl of clay to the highest form of earthenware vase; and from the monotonous strain of African music to the lofty conception of Mozart. But this is a continuity of ideas covering the whole human race as a unit, rather than the progressive development of a single branch of the race.

Consider for a moment the mental and physical environment of the ancient cave or forest dweller. The skies to him were marked only as they affected his bodily comfort in sunshine or storm; the trees invited his attention as they furnished him food or shelter; the roaring torrent was nothing to him except as it obstructed his journey; the sun and the moon and the stars in the heavens filled him with portentous awe, and the spirits in the invisible world worked for his good or for his evil. Beyond his utilitarian senses no art emotion stirred in these signs of creation. Perhaps the first art emotion was aroused in contemplation of the human body. Through vanity, fear, or love he began to decorate it. He scarifies or tattoos his naked body with figures upon his back, arms, legs, and face to represent an idea of beauty. While the tribal or totemic design may have originated the custom, he wishes to be attractive to others, and his first emotions of beauty are thus expressed. The second step is to paint his face and body to express love, fear, hate, war, or religious emotions. This leads on to the art of decorating the body with ornaments, and subsequently to the ornamentation of clothing.

The art of representation at first possessed little artistic beauty, though the decorations on walls of caves show skill in lines and color. The first representations sought only intelligence in communicating thought. The bas-reliefs of the ancients showed skill in representation. The ideal was finally developed until the aesthetic taste was improved, and the Greek sculpture shows a high development of artistic taste. In it beauty and truth were harmoniously combined. The arts of sculpture and painting are based upon the imagination. Through its perfect development, and the improvement in the art of execution, have been secured the aesthetic products of man. Yet there is always a mingling of the emotional nature in the development of fine arts. The growth of the fine arts consists in intensifying the pleasurable sensations of eye and ear. This is done by enlarging the capacity for pleasure and increasing the opportunity for its satisfaction. The beginnings of the fine arts were small, and the capacity to enjoy must have been slowly developed. Of the arts that appeal to the eye there may be enumerated sculpture, painting, drawing, landscape-gardening, and architecture. The pleasure from all except the last comes from an attempt to represent nature. Architecture is founded upon the useful, and combines the industrial and the fine arts in one. The attempt to imitate nature is to satisfy the emotions aroused in its contemplation.

The Love of the Beautiful Slowly Develops.—There must have developed in man the desire to make a more perfect arrow-head, axe, or celt for the efficiency of service, and later for beauty of expression. There must early have developed an idea of good form and bright colors in clothing. So, too, in the mixing of colors for the purpose of expressing the emotions there gradually came about a refinement in blending. Nor could man's attention be called constantly to the beautiful plants and flowers, to the bright-colored stones, metals, and gems found in the earth without developing something more than mere curiosity concerning them. He must early have discovered the difference between objects which aroused desire for possession and those that did not. Ultimately he preferred a more beautifully finished stone implement than one crudely constructed—a more beautiful and showy flower than one that was imperfect, and likewise more beautiful human beings than those that were crude and ugly.

The pleasure of sound manifested itself at an earlier stage than the pleasure of form, although the degree of advancement in music varies in different tribes. Thus the inhabitants of Africa have a much larger capacity for recognizing and enjoying the effect of harmonious sounds than the aborigines of America. While all nations have the faculty of obtaining pleasure from harmonious sounds, it varies greatly, yet not more widely than between separate individuals. It may be considered quite a universal faculty. The love of the beautiful in form, color, and in harmonious sound, is a permanent social force, and has much to do in the progress of civilization. Yet it is not an essential force, for the beginnings of civilization could have been made without it. However, it gives relief to the cold business world; the formal association of men is softened and embellished by painting, poetry, and music. Thus considered, it represents an important part of the modern social development. Art culture, which represents the highest expression of our civilization, has its softening influences on human life.

SUBJECTS FOR FURTHER STUDY

1. The importance of language in the development of culture.

2. Does language always originate the same way in different localities?

3. Does language develop from a common centre or from many centres?

4. What bearing has the development of language upon the culture of religion, music, poetry, and art?

5. Which were the more important impulses, clothing for protection or for adornment?

6. Show that play is an important factor in society-building.

7. Compare pictograph, ideograph, and phonetic writing.

THE SEATS OF EARLY CIVILIZATIONS

CHAPTER VIII

THE INFLUENCE OF PHYSICAL NATURE ON HUMAN PROGRESS

Man Is a Part of Universal Nature.—He is an integral part of the universe, and as such he must ever be subject to the physical laws which control it. Yet, as an active, thinking being, conscious of his existence, it is necessary to consider him in regard to the relations which he sustains to the laws and forces of physical nature external to himself. He is but a particle when compared to a planet or a sun, but he is greater than a planet because he is conscious of his own existence, and the planet is not. Yet his whole life and being, so far as it can be reasoned about, is dependent upon his contact with external nature. By adaptation to physical environment he may live; without adaptation he cannot live.

As a part of evolved nature, man comes into the world ignorant of his surroundings. He is ever subject to laws which tend to sweep him onward with the remaining portions of the system of which he is a part, but his slowly awakening senses cause him to examine his surroundings. First, he has a curiosity to know what the world about him is like, and he begins a simple inquiry which leads to investigation. The knowledge he acquires is adapted to his use day by day as his vision extends. Through these two processes he harmonizes his life with the world about him. By degrees he endeavors to bring the materials and the forces of nature into subjection to his will. Thus he progresses from the student to the master. External nature is unconscious, submitting passively to the laws that control it, but man, ever conscious of himself and his effort, attempts to dominate the forces surrounding him and this struggle to overcome environment has characterized his progress. But in this struggle, nature has reciprocated its influence on man in modifying his development and leaving her impress on him. Limited he has ever been and ever will be by his environment. Yet within the limits set by nature he is master of his own destiny and develops by his own persistent endeavor.

Indeed, the epitome of civilization is a struggle of nature and thought, the triumph of the psychical over the physical; and while he slowly but surely overcomes the external physical forces and makes them subordinate to his own will and genius, civilization must run along natural courses even though its products are artificial. In many instances nature appears bountiful and kind to man, but again she appears mean and niggardly. It is man's province to take advantage of her bounty and by toil and invention force her to yield her coveted treasures. Yet the final outcome of it all is determined by the extent to which man masters himself.

Favorable Location Is Necessary for Permanent Civilization.—In the beginning only those races have made progress that have sought and obtained favorable location. Reflect upon the early civilizations of the world and notice that every one was begun in a favorable location. Observe the geographical position of Egypt, in a narrow, fertile valley bounded by the desert and the sea, cut off from contact with other races. There was an opportunity for the Egyptians to develop continuity of life sufficient to permit the beginnings of civilization. Later, when wealth and art had developed, Egypt became the prey of covetous invading nations. So ancient Chaldea, for a time far removed from contact with other tribes, and protected by desert, mountain, and sea, was able to begin a civilization.

But far more favorable, not only for a beginning of civilization but for a high state of development, was the territory occupied by the Grecian tribes. Shut in from the north by a mountain range, surrounded on every other side by the sea, a fertile and well-watered land, of mild climate, it was protected from the encroachments of "barbarians." The influence of geographical contour is strongly marked in the development of the separate states of Greece. The small groups that settled down on a family basis were separated from each other by ranges of hills, causing each community to develop its own characteristic life. These communities had a common language, differing somewhat in dialect, and the foundation of a common religion, but there never could exist sufficient similarity of character or unity of sentiment to permit them to unite into a strong central nation. A variety of life is evinced everywhere. Those who came in contact with the ocean differed from those who dwelt in the interior, shut in by the mountains. The contact with the sea gives breadth of thought, largeness of life, while those who are enclosed by mountains lead a narrow life, intense in thought and feeling. Without the protection of nature, the Grecian states probably would never have developed the high state of civilization which they reached.

Rome presents a similar example. It is true that the Italian tribes that entered the peninsula had considerable force of character and thorough development as they were about to enter upon a period of civilization. Like the Greeks, the discipline of their early Aryan ancestors had given them much of strength and character. Yet the favorable location of Italy, bounded on the north by a high mountain range and enclosed by the sea, gave abundant opportunity for the national germs to thrive and grow. Left thus to themselves, dwelling under the protection of the snow-capped Alps, and surrounded by the beneficent sea, national life expanded, government and law developed and thrived, and the arts of civilized life were practised. The national greatness of the Romans may in part be attributed to the period of repose in which they pursued unmolested the arts of peace before their era of conquest began.

Among the mountains of Switzerland are people who claim never to have been conquered. In the wild rush of the barbarian hordes into the Roman Empire they were not overrun. They retain to this day their early sentiments of liberty; their greatness is in freedom and equality. The mountains alone protected them from the assaults of the enemy and the crush of moving tribes.

Other nations might be mentioned that owe much to geographical position. More than once in the early part of her history it protected Spain from destruction. The United States, in a large measure, owes her independent existence to the fact that the ocean rolls between her and the mother country. On the other hand, Ireland has been hampered in her struggle for independent government on account of her proximity to

England. The natural defense against enemies, the protection of mountains and forests, the proximity to the ocean, all have had their influence in the origin and development of nations. Yet races, tribes, and nations, once having opportunity to develop and become strong, may flourish without the protecting conditions of nature. They may defy the mountains, seas, and the streams, and the onslaughts of the wild tribes.

The Nature of the Soil an Essential Condition of Progress.—But geography alone, although a great factor in progress, is powerless without a fertile soil to yield a food supply for a large population. The first great impetus of all early civilizations occurred through agriculture. Not until this had developed so as to give a steady food supply were people able to have sufficient leisure to develop the other arts of life. The abundant food supply furnished by the fertility of the Nile valley was the key to the Egyptian civilization. The valley was overflowed annually by the river, which left a fertilizing sediment upon the land already prepared for cultivation. Thus annually without excessive labor the soil was watered, fertilized, and prepared for the seed. Even when irrigation was introduced, in order to obtain a larger supply of food, the cultivation of the soil was a very easy matter. Agriculture consisted primarily in sowing seed on ready prepared ground and reaping the harvest. The certainty of the crop assured a living. The result of cheap food was to rapidly multiply the race, which existed on a low plane. It created a mass of inferior people ruled by a few despots.

What is true of Egypt is true of all of the early civilizations, as they each started where a fertile soil could easily be tilled. The inhabitants of ancient Chaldea developed their civilization on a fertile soil. The great cities of Nineveh and Babylon were surrounded by rich valleys, and the yield of agricultural products made civilization possible. The earliest signs of progress in India were along the valleys of the Ganges and the Indus. Likewise, in the New World, the tribes that approached the nearest to civilization were situated in fertile districts in Peru, Central America, Mexico, and New Mexico.

The Use of Land the Foundation of Social Order.—The manner in which tribes and nations have attached themselves to the soil has determined the type of social organization. Before the land was treated as property of individuals or regarded as a permanent possession by tribes, the method in which the land was held and its use determined the quality of civilization, and the land factor became more important as a determiner of social order as civilization progressed. It was exceedingly important in determining the quality of the Greek life, and the entire structure of Roman civilization was based on the land question. Master the land tenure of Rome and you have laid the foundation of Roman history. The desire for more land and for more room was the chief cause of the barbarian invasion of the empire. All feudal society, including lords and vassals, government and courts, was based upon the plan of feudal land-holding.

In modern times in England the land question has been at times the burning political and economic question of the nation, and is a disturbing factor in recent times. In the United States, rapid progress is due more to the bounteous supply of free, fertile lands than to any other single cause. Broad, fertile valleys are more pertinent as the foundation of nation-building than men are accustomed to believe; and now that nearly all the public domain has been apportioned among the citizens, intense desire for land remains unabated, and its method of treatment through landlord and tenant is rapidly becoming a troublesome question. The relation of the soil to the population presents new problems, and the easy-going civilization will be put to a new test.

Climate Has Much to Do with the Possibilities of Progress.—The early seats of civilization mentioned above were all located in warm climates. Leisure is essential to all progress. Where it takes man all of his time to earn a bare subsistence there is not much room for improvement. A warm climate is conducive to leisure, because its requirements of food and clothing are less imperative than in cold countries. The same quantity of food will support more people in warm than in cold climates. This, coupled with the fact that nature is more spontaneous in furnishing a bountiful supply in warm climates than in cold, renders the first steps in progress much more possible. The food in warm climates is of a light vegetable character, which is easily prepared for use; indeed, in many instances it is already prepared. In cold countries, where it is necessary to consume large amounts of fatty food to sustain life, the food supply is meagre, because this can only be obtained from wild animals. In this region it costs immense labor to obtain sufficient food for the support of life; likewise, in a cold climate it takes much time to tame animals for use and to build huts to protect from the storm and the cold. The result is that the propagation of the race is slow, and progress in social and individual life is retarded.

We should expect, therefore, all of the earliest civilization to be in warm regions. In this we are not disappointed, in noting Egypt, Babylon, Mexico, and Peru. Soil and climate co-operate in furnishing man a suitable place for his first permanent development. There is, however, in this connection, one danger to be pointed out, arising from the conditions of cheap food— namely, a rapid propagation of the race, which entails misery through generations. In these early populous nations, great want and misery frequently prevailed among the masses of the people. Thousands of laborers, competing for sustenance, reduce the earning capacity to a very small amount, and this reduces the standard of life. Yet because food and shelter cost little, they are able to live at a low standard and to multiply rapidly. Human life becomes cheap, is valued little by despotic rulers, who enslave their fellows. Another danger in warm climates which counteracts the tendency of nations to progress, is the fact that warm climates enervate man and make him less active; hence it occurs that in colder climates with unfavorable surroundings great progress is made on account of the excessive energy and strong will-force of the inhabitants.

In temperate climates man has reached the highest state of progress. In this zone the combination of a moderately cheap food supply and the necessity of excessive energy to supply food, clothing, and protection has been most conducive to the highest forms of progress. While, therefore, the civilization of warm climates has led to despotism, inertia, and the degradation of the masses, the civilization of temperate climates has led to freedom, elevation of humanity, and progress in the arts. This illustrates how essential is individual energy in taking advantage of what nature has provided.

The General Aspects of Nature Determine the Type of Civilization.— While the general characteristics of nature have much to do with the development of the races of the earth, it is only a single factor in the great complex of influences. People living in the mountain fastnesses, those living at the ocean side, and those living on great interior plains vary considerably as to mental characteristics and views of life in general. Buckle has expanded this idea at some length in his comparison of India and Greece. He has endeavored to show that "the history of the human mind can only be understood by connecting with it the history and aspects of the material universe." He holds that everything in India tended to depress the dignity of man, while everything in Greece tended to exalt it. After comparing these two countries of ancient civilization in respect to the development of the imagination, he says: "To sum up the whole, it may be said that the Greeks had more respect for human powers; the Hindus for superhuman. The first dealt with the known and available, the second with the unknown and mysterious." He attributes this difference largely to the fact that the imagination was excessively developed in India, while the reason predominated in Greece. The cause attributed to the development of the imagination in India is the aspect of nature.

Everything in India is overshadowed with the immensity of nature. Vast plains, lofty mountains, mighty, turbulent rivers, terrible storms, and demonstrations of natural forces abound to awe and terrify. The causes of all are so far beyond the conception of man that his imagination is brought into play to furnish images for his excited and terrified mind. Hence religion is extravagant, abstract, terrible. Literature is full of extravagant poetic images. The individual is lost in the system of religion, figures but little in literature, and is swallowed up in the immensity of the universe. While, on the other hand, the fact that Greece had no lofty mountains, no great plains; had small rivulets in the place of rivers, and few destructive storms, was conducive to the development of calm reflection and reason. Hence, in Greece man predominated over nature; in India, nature overpowered man.[1]

There is much of truth in this line of argument, but it must not be carried too far. For individual and racial characteristics have much to do with the development of imagination, reason, and religion. The difference, too, in the time of development, must also be considered, for Greece was a later product, and had the advantage of much that had preceded in human progress. And so far as can be determined, the characteristics of the Greek colonists were quite well established before they left Asia. The supposition, also, that man is subject entirely to the influence of physical nature for his entire progress, must be taken with modification. His mind-force, his individual will-force, must be accounted for, and these occupy a large place in the history of his progress. No doubt the thunders of Niagara and the spectacle of the volume of water inspire poetic admiration in the minds of the thousands who have gazed on this striking physical phenomenon of nature. It is awe-inspiring; it arouses the emotions; it creates poetic imagination. But the final result of contact with the will of man is to turn part of that force from its channels, to move the bright machinery engaged in creating things useful and beautiful which contribute to the larger well-being of man.

Granting that climate, soil, geographical position, and the aspects of nature have a vast influence in limiting the possibilities of man's progress, and in directing his mental as well as physical characteristics, it must not be forgotten that in the contact with these it is his mastery over them which constitutes progress, and this involves the activity of his will-power. Man is not a slave to his environment. He is not a passive creature acted upon by sun and storm and subjected to the powers of the elements. True, that there are set about him limitations within which he must ever act. Yet from generation to generation he forces back these limits, enlarges the boundary of his activities, increases the scope of his knowledge, and brings a larger number of the forces of nature in subjection to his will.

Physical Nature Influences Social Order.—Not only is civilization primarily based upon the physical powers and resources of nature, but the quality of social order is determined thereby. Thus, people following the streams, plains, and forests would develop a different type of social order from those who would settle down to permanent seats of agriculture. The Bedouin Arabs of the desert, although among the oldest of organized groups, have changed very little through the passing centuries, because their mode of life permits only a simple organization. Likewise, it is greatly in contrast with the modern nations, built upon industrial and commercial life, with all of the machinery run by the powers of nature. When Rome developed her aristocratic proprietors to whom the land was apportioned in great estates, the old free farming population disappeared and slavery became a useful adjunct in the methods adopted for cultivating the soil. On the other hand, the old village community where land was held in common developed a small co-operative group closely united on the basis of mutual aid. The great landed estates of England and Germany must, so long as they continue, influence the type of social order and of government that will exist in those countries.

As the individual is in a measure subservient to the external laws about him, so must the social group of which he forms a part be so controlled. The flexibility and variability of human nature, with its power of adaptation, make it possible to develop different forms of social order. The subjective side of social development, wherein the individual seeks to supply his own wants and follow the directions of his own will, must ever be a modifying power acting upon the social organization. Thus society becomes a great complex of variabilities which cannot be reduced to exact laws similar to those found in physical nature. Nevertheless, if society in its development is not dependent upon immutable laws similar to those discovered in the forces of nature, yet as part of the great scheme of nature it is directly dependent upon the physical forces that permit it to exist the same as the individual. This would give rise to laws of human association which are modified by the laws of external nature. Thus, while society is psychical in its nature, it is ever dependent upon the material and the physical for its existence. However, through co-operation, man is able to more completely master his environment than by working individually. It is only by mutual aid and social organization that he is able to survive and conquer.

SUBJECTS FOR FURTHER STUDY

1. Give examples coming within your own observation of the influence of soil and climate on the character of society.

2. Does the character of the people in Central America depend more on climate than on race?

3. In what ways does the use of land determine the character of social order?

4. Are the ideals and habits of thought of the people living along the Atlantic Coast different from those of the Middle West? If so, in what respect?

5. Is the attitude toward life of the people of the Dakota wheat belt different from those of New York City?

6. Compare a mining community with an agricultural community and record the differences in social order and attitude toward life.

[1] Henry Thomas Buckle, *History of Civilization in England.* General Introduction.

CHAPTER IX

CIVILIZATION OF THE ORIENT

The First Nations with Historical Records in Asia and Africa.—The seats of the most ancient civilizations are found in the fertile valleys of the Euphrates and the Nile. These centres of civilization were founded on the fertility of the river valleys and the fact of their easy cultivation. Just when the people began to develop these civilizations and whence they came are not determined. It is out of the kaleidoscopic picture of wandering humanity seeking food and shelter, the stronger tribes pushing and crowding the weaker, that these permanent seats of culture became established. Ceasing to wander after food, they settled down to make the soil yield its products for the sustenance of life. Doubtless they found other tribes and races had been there before them, though not for permanent habitation. But the culture of any one group of people fades away toward its origins, mingling its customs and life with those who preceded them. Sometimes, indeed, when a tribe settled down to permanent achievement, its whole civilization is swept away by more savage conquerors. Sometimes, however, the blood of the invaders mingled with the conquered, and the elements of art, religion, and language of both groups have built up a new type of civilization.

The geography of the section comprising the nations where the earliest achievements have left permanent records, indicates a land extending from a territory east of the Tigris and Euphrates westward to the eastern shore of the Mediterranean and southward into Egypt. Doubtless, this region was one much traversed by tribes of various languages and cultures. Emerging from the Stone Age, we find the civilization ranging from northern Africa and skirting Arabia through Palestine and Assyria down into the valley of the Tigris and the Euphrates. Doubtless, the civilization that existed in this region was more or less closely related in general type, but had derived its character from many primitive sources. As history dawns on the achievements of these early nations, it is interesting to note that there was a varied rainfall within this territory. Some parts were well watered, others having long seasonal periods of drought followed by periodical rains. It would appear, too, the uncertainty of rainfall seemed to increase rather than diminish, for in the valley of the Euphrates, as well as in the valley of the Nile, the inhabitants were forced to resort to artificial irrigation for the cultivation of their crops.

It is not known at what time the Chaldeans began to build their artificial systems of irrigation, but it must have been brought about by the gain of the population on the food supply, or perhaps an increased uncertainty of rainfall. At any rate, the irrigation works became a systematic part of their industry, and were of great size and variety. It took a great deal of engineering skill to construct immense ditches necessary to control the violent floods of the Euphrates and the Tigris. So far as evidence goes, the irrigation was carried on by the gravity system, by which canals were built from intakes from the river and extended throughout the cultivated district. In Egypt for a long time the periodical overflow of the Nile brought in the silt for fertilizer and water for moisture. When the flood subsided, seed was planted and the crop raised and harvested. As the population spread, the use of water for irrigation became more general, and attempts were made to distribute its use not only over a wider range of territory but more regularly throughout the seasons, thus making it possible to harvest more than one crop a year, or to develop diversified agriculture. The Egyptians used nearly all the modern methods of procuring, storing, and distributing water. Hence, in these centres of warm climate, fertile land, and plenty of moisture, the earth was made to yield an immense harvest, which made it possible to support a large population. The food supply having been established, the inhabitants could devote themselves to other things, and slowly developed the arts and industries.

Civilization in Mesopotamia.—The Tigris and Euphrates, two great rivers having their sources in mountain regions, pouring their floods for centuries into the Persian Gulf, made a broad, fertile valley along their lower courses. The soil was of inexhaustible fertility and easy of cultivation. The climate was almost rainless, and agriculture was dependent upon artificial irrigation. The upper portion of this great river valley was formed of undulating plains stretching away to the north, where, almost treeless, they furnished great pasture ranges for flocks and herds, which also added to the permanency of the food supply and helped to develop the wealth and prosperity of the country. It was in this climate, so favorable for the development of early man, and with this fertile soil yielding such bountiful productions, that the ancient Chaldean civilization started, which was followed by the Babylonian and Assyrian civilizations, each of which developed a great empire. These empires, ruling in turn, not only represented centres of civilization and wealth, but they acquired the overlordship of territories far and wide, their monarchs ruling eastward toward India and westward toward Phoenicia. In early times ancient Chaldea, located on the lower Euphrates, was divided into two parts, the lower portion known as Sumer, and the other, the upper, known as Akkad. While in the full development of these civilizations the Semitic race was dominant, there is every appearance that much of the culture of these primitive peoples came from farther east.

Influences Coming from the Far East.—The early inhabitants of this country have sometimes been called Turanian to distinguish them from Aryans, Semites, and other races sometimes called Hamitic. They seem to have been closely allied to the Mongolian type of people who developed centres of culture in the Far East and early learned the use of metals and developed a high degree of skill in handicraft. The Akkadians, or Sumer-Akkadians, appear to have come from the mountain districts north and east, and entered this fertile valley to begin the work of civilization at a very early period. Their rude villages and primitive systems of life were to be superseded by civilizations of other races that, utilizing the arts and industries of the Akkadians, carried their culture to a much higher standard. The Akkadians are credited with bringing into this country the methods of making various articles from gold and iron which have been found in their oldest tombs. They are credited with having laid the foundation of the industrial arts which were manifested at an early time in ancient Chaldea, Egypt, and later in Babylonia and Phoenicia. Whatever foundation there may be for this theory, the subsequent history of the civilizations which have developed from Thibet as a centre would seem to attribute the early skill in handiwork in the metals and in porcelain and glass to these people. They also early learned to make inscriptions for permanent record in a crude way and to construct buildings made of brick.

The Akkadians brought with them a religious system which is shown in a collection of prayers and sacred texts found recorded in the ruins at the great library at Nineveh. Their religion seemed to be a complex of animism and nature-worship. To them the universe was peopled with spirits who occupied different spheres and performed different services. Scores of evil spirits working in groups of seven controlled the earth and man. Besides these there were numberless demons which assailed man in countless forms, which worked daily and hourly to do him harm, to control his spirit, to bring confusion to his work, to steal the child from the father's knee, to drive the son from the father's house, or to withhold from the wife the blessings of children. They brought evil days. They brought ill-luck and misfortune. Nothing could prevent their destructiveness. These spirits, falling like rain from the skies to the earth, could leap from house to house, penetrating the doors like serpents. Their dwelling-places were scattered in the marshes by the sea, where sickly pestilence arose, and in the deserts, where the hot winds drifted the sands. Sickness and disease were represented by the demons of pestilence and of fever, which bring destruction upon man. It was a religion of fatalism, which held that man was ever attacked by unseen enemies against whom there was no means of defense. There was little hope in life and none after death. There was no immortality and no eternal life. These spirits were supposed to be under the control of sorcerers and magicians or priests, resembling somewhat the medicine men of the wild tribes of North America, who had power to compel them, and to inflict death or disaster upon the objects of their censure and wrath. Thus, these primitive peoples of early Chaldea were terrorized by the spirits of the earth and by the wickedness of those who manipulated the spirits.

The only bright side of this picture was the creation of other spirits conceived to be essentially good and beneficial, and to whom prayers were directed for protection and help. Such beings were superior to all evil spirits, provided their support could be invoked. So the spirit of heaven and the spirit of earth both appealed to the imagination of these primitive people, who thought that these unseen creatures called gods possessed all knowledge and wisdom, which was used to befriend and protect. Especially would they look to the spirit of earth as their particular protector, who had power to break the spell of the spirits, compel obedience, and bring terror into the hearts of the wicked ones. Such, in brief, was the religious system which these people created for themselves. Later, after the Semitic invasion, a system of religion developed more colossal in its imagination and yet not less cruel in its final decrees regarding human life and destiny. It passed into the purely imaginative religion, and the worship of the sun and moon and the stars gave man's imagination a broader vision, even if it did not lift him to a higher standard of moral conduct.

It is not known at what date these early civilizations began, but there is some evidence that the Akkadians appeared in the valley not less than four thousand years before Christ, and that subsequently they were conquered by the Elamites in the east, who obtained the supremacy for a season, and then were reinforced by the Semitic peoples, who ranged northeast, and, from northern Africa through Arabia, eastward to the Euphrates.[1]

Egypt Becomes a Centre of Civilization.—The men of Egypt are supposed to be related racially to the Caucasian people who dwelt in the northern part of Africa, from whom they separated at a very early period, and went into the Nile valley to settle. Their present racial connection makes them related to the well-known Berber type, which has a wide range in northern Africa. Some time after the departure of the Hamitic branch of the Caucasian race into Egypt, it is supposed that another people passed on beyond, entering Arabia, later spreading over Assyria, Babylon, Palestine, and Phoenicia. These were called the Semites. Doubtless, this passage was long continued and irregular, and there are many intermixtures of the races now distinctly Berber and Arabic, so that in some parts of Egypt, and north of Egypt, we find an Arab-Berber mongrel type. Doubtless, when the Egyptian stock of the Berber type came into Egypt they found other races whose life dates back to the early Paleolithic, as the stone implements found in the hills and caves and graves showed not only Neolithic but Paleolithic culture. Also, the wavering line of Sudan negro types extended across Africa from east to west and came in contact with the Caucasian stock of northern Africa, and we find many negroid intermixtures.

The Egyptians, however, left to themselves for a number of centuries, began rapid ascendency. First, as before stated, their food supply was permanent and abundant. Second, there were inducements also for the development of the art of measurement of land which later led to the development of general principles of measurement. There was observation of the sun and moon and the stars, and a development of the art of building of stone and brick, out of which the vast pyramid tombs of kings were built. The artificers, too, had learned to work in precious stones and metals and weave garments, also to write inscriptions on tombs and also on the papyrus. It would seem as if the civilization once started through so many centuries had become sufficiently substantial to remain permanent or to become progressive, but Egypt was subject to a great many drawbacks. The nation that has the food supply of the world is sooner or later bound to come into trouble. So it appears in the case of Egypt, with her vast food resources and accumulation of wealth; she was eventually doomed to the attacks of jealous and envious nations.

The history of Egypt is represented by dynasties of kings and changes of government through a long period interrupted by the invasion of tribes from the west and the north, which interfered with the uniformity of development. It is divided into two great centres of development, Lower Egypt, or the Delta, and Upper Egypt, frequently differing widely in the character of civilization. Yet, in the latter part of her supremacy Egypt went to war with the Semitic peoples of Babylon and Assyria for a thousand years. It was the great granary of the world and a centre of wealth and culture.

The kings of Egypt were despots who were regarded by the people as gods. They were the head not only of the state but of the religious system, and consequently through this double headship were enabled to rule with absolute sway. The priesthood, together with a few nobles, represented the intellectual and social aristocracy of the country. Next to them were the warriors, who were an exclusive class. Below these came the shepherds and farmers, and finally the slaves. While the caste system did not prevail with as much rigidity here as in India, all groups of people were bound by the influence of class environment, from which they were unable to extricate themselves. Poorer classes became so degraded that in times of famine they were obliged to sell their liberty, their lives, or their labor to kings for food. They became merely toiling animals, forced for the want of bread to build the monuments of kings. The records of Egyptian civilization through art, writing, painting, sculpture, architecture, and the great pyramids, obelisks, and sphinxes were but the records of the glory of kings, built upon the shame of humanity. True, indeed, there was some advance in the art of writing, in the science of astronomy and geometry, and the manufacture of glass, pottery, linens, and silk in the industrial arts. The revelations brought forth in recent years from the tombs of these kings, where were stored the art treasures representing the civilization of the time, exhibit something of the splendors of royalty and give some idea of the luxuries of the civilization of the higher classes. Here were stored the finest products of the art of the times.

The wonders of Egypt were manifested in the structure of the pyramids, which were merely tombs of kings, which millions of laborers spent their lives in building. They represent the most stupendous structures of ancient civilization whose records remain. Old as they appear, as we look backward to the beginning of history, they represent a culminating period of Egyptian art. Sixty-seven of these great structures extended for about sixty miles above the city of Cairo, along the edge of the Libyan Desert. They are placed along the great Egyptian natural burying place in the western side of the Nile valley, as a sort of boulevard of the tombs of kings and nobles. Most of them are constructed of stone, although several are of adobe or sun-dried brick. The latter have crumbled into great conical mountains, like those of the pyramid temples of Babylon.

The largest pyramid, Cheops, rises to a height of 480 feet, having a base covering 13 acres. The historian Herodotus relates that 120,000 men were employed for 20 years in the erection of this great structure. It has never been explained how these people, not yet well developed in practical mechanics, and not having discovered the use of steam and with no use of iron, could have reared these vast structures. Besides the pyramids, great palaces and temples of the kings of Thebes in Upper Egypt rivalled in grandeur the lonely pyramids of Memphis. Age after age, century after century, witnessed the building of these temples, palaces, and tombs. It is said that the palace of Karnak, the most wonderful structure of ancient or modern times, was more than five hundred years in the process of building, and it is unknown how many hundreds of thousands of men spent their lives for this purpose.

So, too, the mighty sphinxes and colossal statues excite the wonder and admiration of the world. Especially to be mentioned in this connection are the colossi of Thebes, which are forty-seven feet high, each hewn from a single block of granite. Upon the solitary plain these mute figures sat, serene and vigilant, keeping their untiring watch through the passage of the centuries.

The Coming of the Semites.—While the ancient civilization at the mouth of the Euphrates had its origin in primitive peoples from the mountains eastward beyond the Euphrates, and the ancient Egyptian civilization received its impetus from a Caucasian tribe of northern Africa, the great civilization from the Mediterranean Sea to the Indus River was developed by the Semites. Westward from the Euphrates, over Arabia, and through Syria to the Mediterranean coast were wandering tribes of Arabs. Perhaps the most typical ancient type of the Semitic race is found in Arabia. In these desert lands swarms of people have passed from time to time over the known world. Their early life was pastoral and nomadic; hence they necessarily occupied a large territory and were continually on the move. The country appears to have been, from the earliest historic records, gradually growing drier—having less regular rainfall.

So these people were forced at times to the mountain valleys and the grasslands of the north, and as far as the agricultural lands in the river valleys, hovering around the settled districts for food supplies for themselves and their herds. After the early settlement of Sumer and Akkad, these Semitic tribes moved into the valley of the Euphrates, and under Sargon I conquered ancient Babylonia at Akkad and afterward extended the conquest south over Sumer. They found two main cities to the west of the Euphrates, Ur and Eridu. Having invaded this territory, they adopted the arts and industries already established, but brought in the dominant power and language of the conquerors. Four successive invasions of these people into this territory eventually changed the whole life into Semitic civilization.

Later a branch moved north and settled higher up on the Tigris, founding the city of Nineveh. The Elamites, another Semitic tribe on the east of the Euphrates, founded the great cities of Susa and Ecbatana. Far to the northwest were the Armenian group of Semites, and directly east on the shores of the Mediterranean were the Phoenicians. This whole territory eventually became Semitic in type of civilization. Also, the Hixos, or shepherd kings, invaded Egypt and dominated that territory for two hundred years. Later the Phoenicians became the great sea-going people of the world and extended their colonies along the coasts through Greece, Italy, northern Africa, and Spain. So there was the Semitic influence from the Pillars of Hercules far east to the River Indus, in India.

Strange to say, the mighty empires of Babylon and Nineveh and Phoenicia and Elam failed, while a little territory including the valley of the Jordan, called Palestine, containing a small and insignificant branch of the Semitic race, called Hebrews, developed a literature, language, and religion which exercised a most powerful influence in all civilizations even to the present time.

The Phoenicians Became the Great Navigators.—While the Phoenicians are given credit for establishing the first great sea power, they were not the first navigators. Long before they developed, boats plied up and down the Euphrates River, and in the island of Crete and elsewhere the ancient Aegeans carried on their trade in ships with Egypt and the eastern Mediterranean. The Aegean civilization preceded the Greeks and existed at a time when Egypt and Babylon were young. The principal city of Cnossus exhibited also a high state of civilization, as shown in the ruins discovered by recent explorers in the island of Crete. It is known that they had trade with early Egypt, but whether their city was destroyed by an earthquake or by the savage Greek pirates of a later day is undetermined. The Phoenicians, however, developed a strip of territory along the east shore of the Mediterranean, and built the great cities of Tyre and Sidon. From these parent cities they extended their trade down through the Mediterranean and out through the Pillars of Hercules, and founded their colonies in Africa, Greece, Italy, and Spain. Long after Tyre and Sidon, the parent states, had declined, Carthage developed one of the most powerful cities and governments of ancient times. No doubt, the Phoenicians deserve great credit for advancing shipbuilding, trade, and commerce, and in extending their explorations over a wide range of the known earth. To them, also, we give credit for the perfection of the alphabet and the manufacture of glass, precious stones, and dyes; but their prominence in history appears in the long struggle between the Carthaginians and the Romans.

A Comparison of the Egyptian and Babylonian Civilizations.—Taken as a whole, there is a similarity in some respects between the Egyptian and the Babylonian civilizations. Coming from different racial groups, from different centres, there must necessarily be contrasts in many of the arts of life. Egypt was an isolated country with a long river flowing through its entire length, which brought from the mountains the detritus which kept its valleys fertile. Communication was established through the whole length by boats, which had a tendency to promote social intercourse and establish national life. With the Mediterranean on the north, the Red Sea on the east, and the Libyan Desert to the west, it was tolerably well protected even though not shut in by high mountain ranges. Yet it was open at all times for the hardy invaders who sought food for flocks and herds and people. There was always "corn in Egypt" to those people suffering from drought in the semi-arid districts of Africa and Arabia.

Nevertheless, while Egypt suffered many invasions, she maintained with considerable constancy the ancient racial traits, and had a continuity of development through the passing centuries which retained many of the primitive characteristics. The valley of the Euphrates was kept fertile by the flow of the great rivers, the Tigris and Euphrates, which, having a large watershed in the mountains, brought floods down through the valleys bearing the silt which made the land fertile. But in both countries at an early period the population encroached upon the natural supply of food, and methods of irrigation were introduced to increase the food supply. The attempts to build palaces, monuments, and tombs were characteristic of both peoples. On account of the dryness of the climate, these great monuments have been preserved with a freshness through thousands of years. In the valley of the Euphrates many of the cities that were reduced to ruin were covered with the drifting sands and floods until they are buried beneath the surface.

In sculpture, painting, and in art, as well as in permanency of her mighty pyramids, sphinxes, and tombs, Egypt stands far ahead of Babylonia. The difference is mainly expressed in action, for in Egypt there is an expression of calm, solemnity, and peace in the largest portions of the architectural works, while in Babylonia there is less skill and more action. The evidences of the type of civilization are similar in one respect, namely, that during the thousand years of development the great monuments were left to show the grandeur of kings, monarchs, and priests, built by thousands of slaves suffering from the neglect of their superiors through ages of toil. Undoubtedly, this failure to recognize the rights of suffering humanity gradually brought destruction upon these great nations. If the strength of a great nation was spent in building up the mighty representations of the glory and power of kings to the neglect of the improvement of the race as a whole, it could mean nothing else but final destruction.

While we contemplate with wonder the greatness of the monuments of the pyramids and the sphinxes of Egypt and the winged bulls of Assyria, it is a sad reflection on the cost of material and life which it took to build them. No wonder, then, that to-day, where once people lived and thought and toiled, where nations grew and flourished, where fields were tilled and harvests were abundant, and where the whole earth was filled with national life, there is nothing remaining but a barren waste and drifting sands, all because men failed to fully estimate real human values and worth. Marvellous as many of the products of these ancient civilizations appear, there is comparatively little to show when it is considered that four thousand years elapsed to bring them about. Mighty as the accomplishments were, the slow process of development shows a lack of vital progress. We cannot escape the idea that the despotism existing in Oriental nations must have crushed out the best life and vigor of a people. It is mournful to contemplate the destruction of these mighty civilizations, yet we may thoughtfully question what excuse could be advanced for their continuance.

It is true that Egypt had an influence on Greece, which later became so powerful in her influences on Western civilizations; and doubtless Babylon contributed much to the Hebrews, who in turn have left a lasting impression upon the world. The method of dispersion of cultures of a given centre shows that all races have been great borrowers, and usually when one art, industry, or custom has been thoroughly established, it may continue to influence other races after the race that gave the product has passed away, or other nations, while the original nation has perished.

The Hebrews Made a Permanent Contribution to World Civilization.— Tradition, pretty well supported by history, shows that Abraham came out of Ur of Chaldea about 1,900 years before Christ, and with his family moved northward into Haran for larger pasture for his flocks on the grassy plains of Mesopotamia. Thence he proceeded westward to Palestine, made a trip to Egypt, and returned to the upper reaches of the Jordan. Here his tribe grew and flourished, and finally, after the manner of pastoral peoples, moved into Egypt for corn in time of drought. There his people lived for several hundred years, attached to the Egyptian nation, and adopting many phases of the Egyptian civilization. When he turned his back upon his people in Babylon, he left polytheism behind. He obtained conception of one supreme being, ruler and creator of the universe, who could not be shown in the form of an image made by man.

This was not the first time in the history of the human race when nations had approximated the idea of one supreme God above all gods and men, but it was the first time the conception that He was the only God and pure monotheism obtained the supremacy. No doubt, in the history of the Hebrew development this idea came as a gradual growth rather than as an instantaneous inspiration. In fact, all nations who have reached any advanced degree of religious development have approached the idea of monotheism, but it remained for the Hebrews to put it in practice in their social life and civil polity. It became the great central controlling thought of national life.

Compared with the great empires of Babylon and Nineveh and Egypt, the Hebrew nation was small, crude, barbarous, insignificant, but the idea of one god controlling all, who passed in conception from a god of authority, imminence, and revenge, to a god of justice and righteousness, who controlled the affairs of men, developed the Hebrew concept of human relations. It led them to develop a legal-ethical system which became the foundation of the Hebrew commonwealth and established a code of laws for the government of the nation, which has been used by all subsequent nations as the foundation of the moral element in their civil code. Moses was not the first lawgiver of the world of nations. Indeed, before Abraham left his ancient home in Chaldea there was ruling in Babylon King Hammurabi, who formulated a wise code of laws, said to be the first of which we have any record in the history of the human race. The Hebrew nation was always subordinate to other nations, but after its tribes developed into a kingdom and their king, Saul, was succeeded by David and Solomon, it reached a high state of civilization in certain lines. Yet, at its best, under the reign of David and Solomon, it was upon the whole a barbarous nation. When the Hebrews were finally conquered and led into captivity in Babylon, they reflected upon their ancient life, their laws, their literature, and there was compiled a greater part of the Bible. This instrument has been greater than the palaces of Babylon or the pyramids of Egypt, or great conquests of military hosts in the perpetuation of the life of a nation. Its history, its religion, its literature in proverbs and songs, its laws, its moral code, all have been enduring monuments that have lasted and will last as long as the human race continues its attempt to establish justice among men.

The Civilizations of India and China.—Before leaving the subject of the Oriental civilizations, at least brief mention must be made of the development of the Hindu philosophy and religion. In the valleys of the great rivers of India, in the shadow of the largest mountains rising to the skies, there developed a great people of great learning and wonderful philosophy. In their abstract conceptions they built up the most wonderful and complex theogony and theology ever invented by men. This system, represented by elements of law, theology, philosophy and language, literature and learning, is found in the Vedas and the great literary remnants of the poets. They reveal to us the intensity of learning at the time of the highest development of the Indian philosophy. However, its influence, wrapped up in the Brahminical religion of fatalism, was largely non-progressive.

Later, about 500 years before Christ, when Gautama Buddha developed his ethical philosophy of life, new hope came into the world. But this did not stay for the regeneration of India, but, rather, declined and passed on into China and Japan. The influence of Indian civilization on Western civilization has been very slight, owing to the great separation between the two, and largely because their objectives have been different. The former devoted itself to the reflection of life, the latter resolved itself into action. Nevertheless, we shall find in the Greek philosophy and Greek religion shadows of the learning of the Orient. But the Hindu civilization, while developing much that is grand and noble, like many Oriental civilizations, left the great masses of the people unaided and unhelped. When it is considered what might have been accomplished in India, it is well characterized as a "land of regrets."

In the dispersion of the human race over the earth, one of the first great centres of culture was found in Thibet, in Asia. Here is supposed to be the origin of the Mongolian peoples, and the Chinese represent one of the chief branches of the Mongolian race. At a very early period they developed an advanced stage of civilization with many commendable features. Their art, the form of pottery and porcelain, their traditional codes of law, were influential in the Far East. Their philosophy culminated in Confucius, who lived about 500 years before Christ, and their religion was founded by Tao Tse, who existed many centuries before. He was the founder of the Taoan religion of China. But the civilization of China extended throughout the Far East, spread into Korea, and then into Japan. It has had very little contact with the Western civilization, and its history is still obscure, but there are many marvellous things done in China which are now in more recent years being faithfully studied and recorded. Their art in porcelain and metals had its influence on other nations and has been of a lasting nature.

The Coming of the Aryans.—The third great branch of the Caucasian people, whose primitive home seems to have been in central Asia, is the Aryan. Somewhere north of the great territory of the Semites, there came gradually down into Nineveh and Babylon and through Armenia a people of different type from the Semites and from the Egyptians. They lived on the great grassy plains of central Asia, wandering with their flocks and herds, and settling down long enough to raise a crop, and then move on. They lived a simple life, but were a vigorous, thrifty, and family-loving people; and while the great civilization of Babylon, Assyria, and Egypt was developing, they were pushing down from the north. They finally developed in Persia a great national life.

Subsequently, under Darius I, a great Aryan empire was established in the seats of the old civilization which he had conquered, whose extent was greater than the world had hitherto known. It extended over the old Assyrian and Babylonian empires, Egypt, Asia Minor, and Syria, in Caucasian and Caspian regions; covered Media and Persia, and extended into India as far as the Indus. The old Semitic civilizations were passing away, and the control of the Aryan race was appearing. Later these Persians found themselves at war with the Greeks, who were of the same racial stock. The Persian Empire was no great improvement over the later Babylonian and Assyrian Empires. It had become more specifically a world empire, which set out to conquer and plunder other nations. It might have been enlightened to a certain extent, but it had received the idea of militarism and conquest. It was the first great empire of the Orient to come in contact with a rising Western civilization, then centering in Greece.

This Aryan stock, when considered in Europe or Western civilization, is known as the Nordic race. In the consideration of Western civilization further discussion will be given of the origin and dispersion of this race.

www.ingramcontent.com/pod-product-compliance
Lightning Source LLC
Chambersburg PA
CBHW080212040426

42333CB00043B/2552